MONEY, MARKETS,
and the $54 HAT

MONEY, MARKETS, and the $54 HAT

what we can learn from taking a new financial perspective

Cory J. Chapman
Managing Partner and CEO of
Elite Financial Center, Inc.

iUniverse, Inc.
New York Lincoln Shanghai

MONEY, MARKETS, and the $54 HAT
what we can learn from taking a new financial perspective

iUniverse books may be ordered through booksellers or by contacting:

iUniverse
2021 Pine Lake Road, Suite 100
Lincoln, NE 68512
www.iuniverse.com
1-800-Authors (1-800-288-4677)

Because of the dynamic nature of the Internet, any Web addresses or links contained in this book may have changed since publication and may no longer be valid.

The information, ideas, and suggestions in this book are not intended to render professional advice. Before following any suggestions contained in this book, you should consult your personal accountant or other financial advisor. Neither the author nor the publisher shall be liable or responsible for any loss or damage allegedly arising as a consequence of your use or application of any information or suggestions in this book.

ISBN: 978-0-595-42454-2 (pbk)
ISBN: 978-0-595-68000-9 (cloth)
ISBN: 978-0-595-86788-2 (ebk)

Printed in the United States of America

This book is dedicated to my wife, who is my best friend and soul mate. Without you in my life, it wouldn't be complete. You have always been my strength when there was no one else to turn to. I will always love you, and I thank God for you every day!

Contents

A Brief Excerpt from Money, Markets, & the $54 Hat

I always tell my clients that arranging their personal finances is a lot like writing a mystery novel: you have to know "whodunit" before you begin writing page one! Whether your ultimate goal is to get out of debt, to save money, or to make good investments—or a combination of all three—you must target your endgame before you even get started on your path toward your ultimate goals.

You must ask yourself honestly and seriously: what is your ultimate goal? What are you trying to get out of this process? Why are you reading this book? Why are you willing to make sacrifices?

Do you intend to save more or to spend more efficiently? To give up or sacrifice? To rework or to discard? Until you answer these questions for yourself, honestly and with clarity, there's really not much that I—or anyone else, for that matter—can do for you.

My clients all have different goals and dreams. Some of these are realistic given the clients' current earning potential or debt load, some less so. Regardless, I frequently hear the same aspirations:

"I want a new house."
"I want to quit work and go back to school."
"I need a new car."
"I'd like to travel to Rome this summer."
"We're looking for a vacation home."
"I want to start putting money away for the kids."

Sometimes the dreams are a little far-fetched for a person's current financial situation. It's hard, for example, to invest in stocks and bonds when you're still getting troubling calls from collection agencies because of bounced checks and maxed-out credit cards. But debt—no matter how big—can be managed. Progress can be made, money can be saved, and you can begin—right now, today—the process of investing in your own personal financial future.

The first thing I'll suggest to you is the first thing I suggest to each and every client who sits at my desk: putting yourself in your own personal financial driver's seat means knowing where you want to go before you get in the car.

You wouldn't think of taking a road trip without a final destination in mind, would you? Knowing where you're going helps you plan for the journey. It helps you budget for gas, pack the cooler, pick out the roadmaps, and put air in the tires.

Keeping this in mind, why do you think you can start investing money before you've settled your debt? Or save for your child's college fund if you have to bounce a check to buy them shoes?

Setting unrealistic financial goals is like trying to drive from Los Angeles to New York on half a tank of gas. You just can't get to your final destination without proper planning, and the first thing you must plan for is where you want to go in the first place.

Acknowledgments

I would like to thank the following people for inspiring me to write this book. First, I would like to thank God Almighty, for without him there is no life! Next, I thank my two boys, Chase and Chance, for motivating me every morning to be a better person and to want to make a better world for them to grow up in. And last but definitely not least, I would like to thank Rusty, who has helped me put my thoughts on paper and pushed me to finish this project. Loyalty is very important to me, and I will never forget you!

Foreword

"Four out of 10 people aged 55 or older,
have less than $100,000 saved toward their retirement."
—2004 Retirement Confidence Survey,
Employee Benefit Research Institute

His clients include top athletes and celebrities, so what can the CEO of one of LA's hottest financial planning firms possibly have to say to you? Plenty. After all, his firm isn't named *Elite* Financial Center for nothing. Cory Chapman has spent nearly thirteen years in the financial sector helping people just like you live extraordinary lives by giving outside-the-box advice.

While his boutique agency might cater to the rich and the powerful, his cachet and influence allow him to spend most of his days sitting across from ordinary people facing everyday concerns. These days, there are plenty of both. With Social Security threatening to be depleted, 401(k)s losing their cachet, and the real estate bubble liable to burst at any minute, average American citizens are more worried than ever about the challenges they face as they confront their uncertain financial future.

Cory Chapman—career financial advisor, consultant, public speaker, and now author of the new book *Money, Markets, & the $54 Hat: What We Can Learn from Taking a New Financial Perspective*—doesn't take the bold claims of his ambitious subtitle lightly. Over the years, he has watched a battle of extremes dominate the financial markets—either investors are given advice that is too aggressive, or they are advised to play it too safe.

As a result, Mr. Chapman is much sought-after for the personalized, sensitive, and, most importantly, tailor-made advice given to a wide range of loyal clients. There is no secret to his success. Rather, it stems from a firm commitment to helping people make use of their most important assets and teaching them to stick to a specific, regimented, and, most of all, *consistent* plan of attack.

It is his recognition of the importance of consistency, in fact, that makes up the core content of *Money, Markets, & the $54 Hat*. Cory likens his role as a financial planner to that of a fitness trainer. Just as a gym's clients need help losing weight, Cory's clients need help gaining assets. Both types of professional must emphasize one trait that is essential for success: "Consistency! Consistency! Consistency!"

The way Cory sees it, most Americans are making enough money; they simply are not motivated enough to do something—*anything*—constructive with it. Some of them wait until it is too late—often just a few years before retirement—and then expect him to work miracles. Others come to him with so much debt that it will take years for them to see returns on any of the investments he suggests.

Still, Cory asserts, it is never too late—and certainly never too early—to begin planning for one's financial future. The keys are to figure out where you are, decide where you want to be, measure the difference, and start doing something about it.

"Just start," says the author. "If I had one piece of advice for people it would be that: just start. Whatever it is, start doing it. Budgeting, investing, researching, analyzing—just start doing something, because the minute you start doing something, it will always lead to something else."

On the surface, this advice may seem simplistic, but Cory is quick to point out that, often, half the problem in financial planning is what he likes to call the "fear factor." He explains, "Everyone's so afraid these days—afraid that Social Security's going to run out; afraid that their homes won't be worth half as much tomorrow as they were worth yesterday; afraid that they won't have enough. I give simple advice because that's what I know works for my clients. They don't believe it when I finish explaining what they need to do, and they ask, 'It's that simple?' But it's not the solution that's difficult, it's sticking to it."

To help readers of this book stick to a firm financial plan that's right for them, Cory will teach them:

- How to avoid the common pitfalls of bad credit

- How to budget when they think there's nothing *to* budget

- The basics of such sound investment tools as stocks, bonds, and mutual funds

- The pros and cons of various products on the market, including IRAs, insurance, and annuities

- How to incorporate their own LLCs to avoid or reduce taxes

  And this is only a partial list.

It is the author's belief that financial planning doesn't have to be difficult. His informal and simple advice will help you make more money than you ever thought possible by doing less than you ever imagined, whether you're just getting out of college, starting to put your children through college, or even going back to college!

No matter what stage of the game you're at, author and financial whiz Cory Chapman will make sure you *start playing today*. For, once you start playing, he believes you'll keep playing until you meet your own personalized definition of "financial success."

Introduction
What Can a $54 Hat Teach Us About Retirement Planning?

"Mr. Chapman?" It was the voice of my assistant.

"Yes?" I asked, looking up from the stack of packing boxes that threatened to overwhelm me at any moment.

"Mrs. Jones is here to see you."

I smiled, and a few seconds later, my favorite "little old lady," as she liked to call herself, strode in on heels as high as her hopes for the future.

"Mrs. Jones!" I said. I flipped down the cuffs of my sleeves and switched from mover mode to mover and shaker mode. "Please," I told her, "have a seat."

I was closing in on my last day of work at one of the mid-eighties' top financial planning firms. Regrets? I had a few, but they were all behind me, and now I was looking forward to the future—to *my* future. I'd made my bones with the company, learned the ropes, and mastered the products, facts, figures, forms, and procedures. Now it was time to branch out on my own.

Even though the firm had reassigned much of my caseload to its other brokers, I still had a few diehard clients coming to see me during those last few days at the office. Mrs. Jones was one of them. As always, she looked prim, proper, and determined. I had always admired the way she dressed up when she came to see me, although I was far from flattered—she no doubt dressed as elegantly to do her grocery shopping or pay her electric bill.

Like many of my clients, Mrs. Jones had been raised in an era in which the advice of a financial planner was as important, if not more so, than that of a doctor, pharmacist, friend, or relative. Having lived through the Great Depression, she knew what it felt like to go without and was fiercely insistent upon never doing so again.

At seventy-eight, Mrs. Jones was facing a critical juncture in her life. Although she was better off than many Americans her age, she instinctively knew that if she didn't plan well for her remaining twenty or thirty years, she'd soon be living hand to mouth. This was something she was desperate to avoid.

She quickly came to the reason for her visit. It had been suggested by friends, family, and her former financial planner that Mrs. Jones take the $100,000 she'd just come into and pay off the remaining mortgage on her house, an amount that happened to total approximately $100,000.

On paper, this seemed like an appropriate thing for her to do. Mrs. Jones could pay off her house and live off her Social Security checks for the rest of her life. She would have no debt, no mortgage, no muss, and no fuss. In the late eighties, this would have been the advice that most analysts at any firm, including mine, would have given Mrs. Jones.

But I *knew* Mrs. Jones. To me, she was more than just a case file or asset checklist. I'd sat across from her and her children many times and learned how she lived—comfortably, but not lavishly. She had to scrimp and save for "the little joys," as she called them, that populated her life. She was then living check to check, and her biggest desire was to buy a $54 hat for spring that she couldn't afford.

But I knew that if she *didn't* pay off the house and capitalized on her equity instead by reorganizing some assets and looking at her financial future from a different perspective—one she found dubious at first—she could do more than survive from Social Security check to Social Security check. She could finally *thrive*.

Mrs. Jones listened to me that day. At first, there were a few frowns and some shaking of the head, but there gradually came to be a nod or two as well. I don't know what made me feel so free with her that day. Perhaps I thought that she'd listen, shake her head, and go to the financial planner next door. Maybe the fact that I was soon to branch out on my own gave me confidence I'd lacked before. Most of all, though, I knew that I was right—I was giving the right advice at the right time to the right client.

At last, Mrs. Jones nodded in understanding.

At last, she agreed with me.

In fact, she became my first client!

I decided to talk to her children to see what their concerns were for their mother. Mrs. Jones had been thinking the way most people think: she had planned to pay off her house and leave it to her children. But she had never bothered to ask them whether that was what *they* wanted. In fact, what they wanted was to see their mom live more comfortably, do some traveling, and actually *enjoy* her retirement years rather than simply endure them.

By the time we had finished reevaluating her financial goals and assessing her assets, she was able to refinance her property (currently worth $1.6 million), increase her cash flow, and restructure her investment portfolio to include high-yielding, guaranteed annuities. As a result, she now lives comfortably on $3,500 in liquid assets each month and has a very nice portfolio that has an average annual return of 10 percent.

And what was the first thing she bought after her finances had been reorganized?

You guessed it: that $54 hat!

I haven't told you this story to take myself down memory lane, to brag about how skilful I am, or even to get Mrs. Jones to write the Foreword to this book! (Hardly, since that's not even her real name.) I've told you this story because it serves to accentuate one of my main points: that each of us is unique. We each have unique incomes, debts, and personalities. We also have our individual comfort zones, to which we cling tightly.

My job as a financial planner is more than just giving my clients advice. My job also includes getting to know them, both personally and professionally. Otherwise, they might as well be getting advice from a nameless, faceless voice on the phone or a Web site on the Internet. Financial planning does not exist in a vacuum—you can't insert income and debt amounts into a formula to get a guaranteed investment strategy that works for everyone, every time.

You have to know how a person lives before you can tell them how to spend, save, invest, buy, or sell. If I hadn't known that Mrs. Jones couldn't afford that $54 hat—not even with all of her assets, choice, and opportunity—I never could have given her the advice I did.

Now, I don't know you, and you don't know me. But I *can* get you to know yourself, and, if you allow me to, I can help you to make the right decisions based on your unique circumstances, so that you can enjoy not just an income but "gross income." So that you can *Make More Money Than You Ever Thought Possible Doing Less Than You Ever Imagined.*

1

Your Invitation to Join The 5 Percent Club

"A vision without a task is but a dream;
"A task without a vision is drudgery;
"A vision with a task is the hope of the world ... "
—**Inscription on a church in Sussex, England, circa 1730**

Since I work with money, I need to be continually aware of the latest national statistics regarding debt, inflation, tax reform, earning potential, and many other critical factors. While I don't want to waste any time boring you with facts and figures, I would like to share with you a statistic that startled even me: in the United States, only 5 percent of the population earns over $100,000 a year.

It's startling, I know. In the wealthiest nation on the planet, in the wealthiest time in our country's history, we're not quite as wealthy as we had all thought. Of course, this is far from the common perception. We all think we're earning more than we really are. What's more, we all tend to think that everybody else is earning *twice* as much as we are.

We look at our neighbor's new car and assume he got a raise. We hear with envy the square footage of our brother-in-law's new (vacation) house and how many tens of thousands of dollars it has increased in value since he bought it. We watch TV shows in which coffee-shop waitresses and out-call masseuses share apartments in downtown Manhattan that would rent for $5,000 a month.

Why is there such a disconnect? How can our perception that we're all raking in the cash be so far from the actual, documented truth that only a tiny fraction of us are really doing so? And—the biggest question of all—what is it about that 5 percent of the population—I call us the 5 Percent Club, and I'm proud to say that I'm a member—that makes them earn more than the other 95 percent? What are they doing right that we're all doing wrong? (And how can we quit doing the wrong things and start doing the right things?)

I'm lucky in that I work with many members of that elite 5 Percent Club every single day and have learned so much from them that I'm now able to share some of that knowledge with you. While I haven't interviewed them all, programmed their particulars into a computer, and calculated specific instructions for you, I *can* tell you one of their important "secrets:" each of them has a specific mind-set that the other 95 percent of us, for the most part, don't share.

The members of the 5 Percent Club are instinctively able to form clear-cut goals, assess how to achieve them, and then, simply … *achieve them*. Whether theirs is a five-week plan, a five-month plan, or a five-year plan, they each have an indubitable, irrevocable, and unyielding *plan* that acts as their own personal roadmap to a level of financial success that few of us ever attain.

So, the bad news is that they're currently doing something we're not.

And the good news?

It's simple, really: we can *all* do the exact same thing.

To join the 5 Percent Club does not require a high tolerance for risk or a high IQ. It does not require a huge starting bankroll, a budget that would make a Tibetan monk cringe or a rich uncle with deep pockets and a blank check with your name on it. To join the 5 Percent Club simply requires one thing: a plan.

You need a plan that is tailored to your needs and circumstances—one that is within your comfort zone when it comes to critical factors like setting a budget, curbing debt, and making firm decisions.

Of course, the plan is just the club's initiation fee. To actually be a part of the exclusive 5 Percent Club—to make over $100,000 a year consistently and comfortably—requires sticking to the plan and having the conviction to reach your vision through the simple tasks that your plan lays out for you.

Reflect on the quote I used at the beginning of this chapter. *A vision without a task is but a dream*. Let's face it, we both have the same vision. Otherwise, you wouldn't be reading my book, and I wouldn't be writing it. Our shared vision is to *make more money*.

Whether it's billions or millions, hundreds of thousands or tens of thousands, we know we don't have enough, and we want to make more. That's our vision. But without a series of tasks—without a set, specific plan of goals to establish, reassess, and then accomplish—that vision will always remain "but a dream."

The 5 Percent Club doesn't just dream; they *do*. They match their visions to their tasks, and they move toward their goals feverishly, with enthusiasm and assurance, until they reach them. Then they reassess their goals, reset the bar a tad higher, and start all over again.

That's another thing about the 5 Percent Club: they know that life is a journey, not a destination. I've never heard a member of the 5 Percent Club say to me, "That's it! That's enough, Cory. I don't need to set any more goals or earn any more interest or vigorously research my investments or buy any more home finance software or add to my children's trust funds or …" As soon as they reach their latest financial goal, they move on to the next, and the next, and the next.

For the 5 Percent Club, the journey is always part of the original plan. No journey begins without a roadmap, and what is a roadmap but a carefully laid out plan that takes into account things like the weather, gas prices, time of year, speed limits, and other variables? And, just like a traveler, a financial planner must keep in mind an Estimated Time of Arrival (ETA).

One nice thing about roadmaps is that they suggest very clear beginnings and equally clear-cut endings. Sure, you may wander a bit while you're on the trip—take in a roadside attraction or break for a rest stop or two along the way—but you always begin at one point and end at another. In this book, we're going to be working on your financial roadmap, including your ETA.

Your journey begins now.

Starting from Where You Are

(And Getting To Where You Want To Be)

Your journey started the minute you picked up this book. You've already begun your travels. This is cause for great joy and celebration, but I caution you not to pop that first bottle of champagne just yet. You're barely halfway to the starting line. After all, you can read and think and ponder all day long, but until you actually get on the freeway—until the rubber finally hits the road—you're really just idling in neutral.

Our problem with starting anything new is universal: we fear the unknown. We have been taught that fear is bad, but financial advisors like myself know that when it comes to taking control of your money matters, fear is often in fact *good*. Fear can inspire growth. I have this helpful piece of advice for the would-be investor: if you're afraid, nervous, and apprehensive, you must be doing *something* right.

Fear of the unknown is both a blessing and a curse. It keeps us from risking too much, but it often keeps us from risking anything at all. No investment is without risk, but facing your fear—embracing your fear—is the first step to creating your own personal roadmap to investment success.

You are right to be afraid. No matter what your friends, relatives, neighbors, and colleagues have made with their financial advisors—be it in real estate, the stock market, or one of the nearly five thousand mutual funds on the market today—there's no such thing as a "sure thing." But every lesson you learn from this book will provide you with another reason to be less afraid. Knowledge is power, and the more knowledge one has, the fewer reasons one has to be afraid.

That's one reason I wrote this book. I've seen too many colleagues hesitate and lose out on good deals. I've seen too many partners talk about pie-in-the-sky earnings only to fall short because they avoided risk and played it safe. I've seen far too many potential clients stay out of the financial game altogether simply because they were too afraid to *just get started*.

I don't want that to happen to you any more than I wanted it to happen to them. We all need to enjoy—yes, *enjoy*—a healthy amount of fear. But fear is only beneficial if it results in caution, not prevention. We don't want to be so scared to take that first step that we never even walk out the door.

You've already taken the first step by buying this book. Now you need to maintain your momentum by realizing that your dreams of personal financial success will never truly become a reality unless you match your singular vision with a specific set of tasks that you know you will be able to accomplish.

Don't wait until you've saved up x number of dollars or read x number of books. Start now—*today*—regardless of your starting point. There will never be a better time than this very moment to get started, because there's never a better time to get started than the present.

As I write this chapter, the first half of January has passed, and some of my resolutions for a bright New Year already lie behind me. I wonder what would happen if we really kept our resolutions. How would our lives change? How much weight could we lose, cigarettes could we not smoke, money could we save, or precious moments could we spend with our families if we could simply make a resolution and *stick to it?*

Think about the resolutions you made last January. Did you keep any of them? Did any of them last past, say, January 12th? Did you lose more than a few pounds, stop smoking for more than a few days, or save more than just enough money to take yourself out for one big dinner?

I'm proud to say that I *did* stick to an important resolution this year. Do you know what it was? It was to write this book. It wasn't easy, but I did it. And this is how I've become a card-carrying member of the 5 Percent Club: by trying as hard as I can to keep the promises I make to myself. Every year, it gets a little easier to keep my resolutions because keeping them in the past has brought so many rewards.

But what about you? What's preventing you from keeping *your* resolutions? Perhaps there aren't enough rewards that you can actually see—not enough of a payoff. But just think of what might have happened if you *had* committed to a resolution that might have affected your financial future in a positive way. It could have been something as simple and painless as giving up that outrageously expensive coffee drink you have on your way to work every morning. You know, the one that costs $3.95 but comes with a free straw? Four dollars a day might not sound like much, but it adds up. If, on New Year's Day of last year, you had resolved to go without that luxury beverage, a year later you would have been $1,460 richer—not to mention a few pounds lighter.

That, my friends, is how the 5 Percent Club makes $100,000 a year and then some. They make resolutions, and they stick to them. They say "I'm going to do *x*, *y*, or *z*," and then—wonder of wonders—they actually *do* it. They don't make excuses; they don't wait until tomorrow; they don't rationalize, justify, or waffle. Whenever they start a task, they stick with it until it has been completed.

Right now, we're probably both feeling a small dose of healthy fear—me because I've never written a book before, and you because you've never invested in your own financial future before. Well, that's good—that's *great*. We're already on the same page! I suspect, though, that with each page we turn together, we'll both grow less afraid and more excited about our journeys.

Our next step will be to talk a little about *you*.

Your Personal Roadmap to Financial Success

(And Why You Shouldn't Be Afraid of Detours)

Just as we have made resolutions that we've neglected or planned diets that we've abandoned, many of us have considered trips that we've never taken—short trips, long trips, foreign trips, domestic trips, romantic trips, adventurous trips, family trips, solo trips. Fear is one reason we miss out on such travel, lack of money is another, and bad timing is still one more. But I suspect that the main reason we put off such trips is our inherent habit of procrastination.

We've been meaning to go all our lives, but something has always prevented us. We have as many excuses for why we didn't go as we had opportunities to go. But procrastination is the true cause of our failure to embark.

Investing, saving, budgeting … these are all tasks that we know we should do, but often don't. Why not? For the same reason we skip those trips we've always been meaning to take: too much fear and not enough money or time. This presents a considerable problem: if we can procrastinate about something fun and exciting like a trip, what hope do we have of getting around to something as dry and stale as investing in our own financial future?

I'm not going to frighten you with sobering statistics (although I certainly could) or appeal to your baser instincts like greed (although I probably should). You and I both know that we could all be doing more to prepare for our own financial futures. You can't walk out the door, turn on the radio or TV, read a paper, or eavesdrop in the elevator without hearing bad news about Social Security, the economy, a pending recession, the real estate market, or the stock market.

You already know that there is risk in the world. What you need to learn is that where there's smoke, there's usually fire. In the case of your finances, your hose will be about a thousand feet too short if you don't take action immediately. It is time for you to risk taking your journey. It is time to take out your own personal roadmap, put your finger on Point A, and trace out your route to Point Z.

Don't worry if you get sidetracked along the way. That's the thing about roadmaps—they sometimes lead us to forget that there's a giant ball of twine fifty miles into our trip, that we had wanted to visit a great little roadside barbecue just around the bend, or that our kids might need to go to the bathroom every fifteen minutes. Life is unpredictable. Emergencies arise, brushfires flare, and unanticipated expenses threaten to derail our careful financial plans.

Don't be afraid to take detours. Budgets are important but not written in stone. There's a reason why your checkbook doesn't come just with deposit slips but with ways to withdraw your money as well.

You might not reach your goal tomorrow, next week, next month, or next year. There may be too many balls of twine or barbecue stands or rest stops along the way for your voyage to be a perfectly smooth one. The important thing is that you get out your map, pack your bags, start the car, and pull out of the driveway.

Remember your resolutions. If you'd started your journey to financial freedom at this time last year, who knows where you'd be by now? Now fast-forward to this time next year and think about how far along life's financial road you could get if you were to start your journey—and stick with it—right now. *Today.*

Mind Your Own Business!

"Mind your own business!"

This is something I tell my clients every day. At first, this causes more than its share of raised eyebrows, but after my clients spend a little time getting to know me, they usually thank me for being so blunt—often during our very first meeting together. Of course, I'm not telling them to "butt out." In fact, it's quite the opposite—I'm actually telling them to butt *in*—into their own financial affairs, that is.

Trusting your financial advisor—any financial advisor, including myself—implicitly, blindly, and completely is no more advisable than putting blind faith in your government, mayor, police force, Social Security, bank, or doctor.

We must learn to mind our own business. In other words, we must learn to accept personal responsibility for our own actions and keep a close watch on our own financial affairs so that there are no surprises, unknown terms, or confusing figures.

I realize that financial planning is about as fun for most people as going to the dentist, but you should realize that it's just as vital to your overall personal well-being. Many of my clients are quite insistent about me helping them save, invest, make, or grow their money. They want *me* to get to work for them as soon as possible.

I understand and respect that.

But I'm equally insistent that *they* do their homework as well.

Do Your Homework!

Most of my clients blanch when I give them their first homework assignment. Some of them even think that I'm joking. Actually, I couldn't be more serious. Since I'm going to be investing their money, I believe that it's critical that they know exactly what I'll be doing with it, how I plan to do it, and, most importantly, *why* I'll be doing it.

I know that a lot of that (okay, *all* of that) is my job, but there's a reason why they call me a financial adviser—I give advice. And I believe that my advice is best heeded when my clients understand exactly what I'm talking about. So I give them homework, and they had better do it. If they don't, the only ones they're cheating are themselves.

One of the first things I recommend is that they invest fifty or sixty dollars in *Microsoft Money* or Intuit's *Quicken* financial software. These programs are available everywhere, and my clients can usually pick them up at any number of places on the way home from their first visit to my office. The best thing about these simple programs is that they allow people to track and understand spending, monitor and schedule bills, [and] automatically generate easy-to-read reports, registers and budgets."

Not only do these programs get them comfortable with working on their computers—an absolute must for staying current and relevant in today's fast-paced world of financial upgrades—but the software also gets them excited about seeing their finances represented in vibrant colors and three-dimensional shapes on their own home computer screens.

I encourage my clients to freely explore their software program of choice, to feel free to make mistakes with imaginary money, and thereby enable themselves to work through their fear. Some of the software's more complicated features can be a bit intimidating at first, but once my clients get the hang of them, they've already completed half of their homework assignment—getting excited about managing their own money.

Their next homework assignment is to figure out a portfolio—to pick a few stocks and research them thoroughly. "I want you to tell me not just the company you pick," I say, "but also why you like the stock. Tell me its gains and losses over the past three-to-five-year period." Working with "play money" not only helps them better understand the kinds of trades and investments I'll be making for them, but it helps them get their feet wet. Quite frankly, this is the point at which many of them get hooked on playing a more active role when it comes to investing their money.

The thing you have to remember about the homework assignment is this: you have to understand how I'm going to help you before I can actually help you. Knowledge is key. Therefore, so is homework.

We've talked a lot about fear, but now it's time to start talking about something even more important: courage. It's not easy to make money in the financial sector, despite what you may have heard from your friends, colleagues, family, or complete strangers in an elevator. You must be willing to learn new things, take risks, and work very, very hard. I like to tell my clients that planning for their financial future is like going to college: you've got to spend four solid years doing hard work before you're ready to venture out on your own. Of course, in reality, financial planning is more like a paid internship—you'll be making money as you learn, and the more you learn, the more you'll make.

Four years sounds like a long time, but it's all relative. Some of us took less time to get our degrees, others took longer, and still others had to settle for a graduate degree from the School of Hard Knocks! In any case, success won't happen overnight. But relax—this is good news. Fast change is rarely lasting change.

I don't want you to read this book excitedly over the course of a few weeks only to wind up frustrated and failing in a few months because I promised you the moon, then took back your telescope. We've all been disappointed by promises of miraculous change, haven't we? We've bought some diet, investing, pop psychology, or get-rich-quick book promising to make us thin, beautiful, happy, or rich overnight, only to find the same old information simply having been rehashed and repackaged in order to call itself "new and improved."

The information I'm going to share with you may not be entirely new, but it's certainly improved. You won't find a lot of pie charts, graphs, facts, or figures in this book. What you *will* find are examples of how you can make your money work for you—in the real world and in real time—without getting lost in a jumble of forms, loopholes, cons, or scams.

But first, you must start to lose your sense of fear.

The first step to eliminating fear from your investment equation is to arm yourself with as much knowledge as possible. Research is the missing ingredient from many a failed investor's already-doomed road trip. When investing, it is important for you to control as many variables as you can. The economy, politics, natural disasters, interest rates, and property values are all variables you *can't* control, no matter how hard you try. However, your knowledge about all of these factors *can* be controlled, merely by researching your own financial future, which must obviously start with your very real and perhaps unpleasant financial *present*.

In the remainder of this chapter, we'll talk about research, and lots of it. Your first step was buying this book, and in so doing, you became the second half of a team. You and I must work together to achieve the success you desire. This requires that you do your homework, and here is where you start.

The Internet

No tool has revolutionized the world of personal finance—not to mention just about every other field—like the Internet. This may come as no surprise to you, but I think that as we explore this handy tool more fully in this section, you *will* be surprised at some of the ways in which the Internet can help you come to grips with your own financial future.

Learning about various issues that affect your bottom-line income, savings, budget, or profit can be quickly and easily achieved by going online to learn the definitions of such basic terms as "loss leader," "portfolio," "low-yield," "budget," "credit," "debt," and so on.

The best place to start? My own website, of course, which can be found at www.efcfinancialcenter.com. Here, in addition to learning more about me, you'll find valuable resources in my "Learning Center," which boasts a slew of financial articles, a finance calculator, a free e-newsletter, e-seminars, and an extensive glossary of the terms you'll need to understand to make informed decisions about your money.

Once you've read the articles that interest you and fiddled with the calculator for a while, you can branch out by using my extensive links section to continue your economic education.

Your Home Office

To consistently and effectively keep up with your homework, you must feel comfortable where you're doing it. Surfing the Internet, sorting through financial statements, or even reading the latest copy of your favorite financial magazine will require many hours in seating positions that might become uncomfortable. This is why you should devote a little time, effort, and expense to creating a home office that suits your needs.

I'm not talking about attaching a new wing to your house here. You don't even have to give up your garage, broom closets, or pool house. Chances are, in fact, that you already have a basic office setup featuring a desk, personal computer, printer, and—if you're anything like me—a handy dictionary and a thesaurus or two.

What I'm suggesting is that you should have a quiet, private, and studious place for serious, focused work. You will need many hours of unbroken study time to make your homework pay off, and if you're located in the midst of a heavy traffic pattern in your house—if your kids constantly stomp by or your spouse feels free to invite you for a snack or to watch television—then the quality of your work will suffer considerably.

Furthermore, the kind of research you'll be doing can become addictive. It's one thing to casually look up a hot stock tip or the latest interest rates, but when you have tens of thousands of dollars of potential profit on the line, your task takes on a whole new aspect. You may find myself working at all hours of the day or night—very early in the morning or after midnight—and it wouldn't be considerate of you to have your computer set up the master bedroom or just outside the kids' rooms.

Therefore, you'll need to find a nice, quiet, and, above all, *private* place for your home office. It will have to be a place where a desk lamp, high-speed internet sounds, and a constantly clacking keyboard won't disturb your family. Don't worry if this requires some creative housekeeping or a little compromise on your family's part—that first fat paycheck, dividend, or jump in your savings account will be all they need to see the logic behind the furniture-shuffling!

Your home office will require a few basic tools: a computer with Internet access; a color printer with plenty of paper and ink cartridges; at least one book-shelf on which to catalog your local resources as well as books like this one; a sturdy and comfortable chair; office supplies like CD-ROMs, paperclips, a sta-pler, highlighters, and sticky-note pads; and enough file folders and accordion wallets to help organize your various financial and bank statements, cancelled checks, budget updates, IRA printouts, tax returns, receipts, and other docu-ments.

If you don't have a lot of room in your office, try to make the space as efficient and clutter-free as possible. If the room is uncomfortable at first, do your best to make it comfortable as time goes on. I want this room to be an oasis for you, a place where you can get creative, do good work, and, above all, put yourself in a mind-set of making lots of money. You simply won't be able to keep up with your research if it's too noisy to hear yourself think.

Like I said, this doesn't have to be a big construction project requiring you to max out your Home Depot card. It doesn't have to be fancy, just efficient. Truth be told, my own main workstation—where I do most of my mapping, plotting, planning, calculating, and highlighting—is a twenty-dollar folding picnic table I got at Office Depot three years ago. It's not fancy, but it's sturdy—and it works for me. I've got plenty of elbow room, and it really allows me the flexibility I need to stretch out and find just what I'm looking for within arm's reach.

It also doesn't hurt if the room is appealing to the senses. If a fresh coat of paint is in order, go for it. If some new posters, throw pillows or area rugs will make you more comfortable, then indulge yourself. For months, I toiled away without so much as a radio, until I got a portable CD player for my birthday and found that having a little smooth jazz playing in the background did wonders for my productivity.

For at least the next few months, your home office is going to be your home away from home (inside your home), so you might as well enjoy the surround-ings. This will both calm your senses and help you get your work done.

A Chapter Ends

(But Your Homework Doesn't)

Think of this chapter as the first leg of your personal journey to a new and satisfy-ing financial future. Every trip starts with a roadmap, and this chapter is yours. Here you have found your essential tools. This chapter has been the gateway to the knowledge you will need in order to begin investing in that most important of all financial sectors: yourself.

The chapter may be over, but your homework never ends. Your journey will last a lifetime, and whether you're starting at the age of twenty, forty, sixty, or eighty, there will always be money to worry about, investments to make, budgets to adhere to, and goals to achieve. I hope that, after reading this introductory chapter, you are looking forward more than ever to your journey.

I've said it before, and I'll say it again: financial planning is investing. Like most people—like myself for many years—you've probably had your head buried in the sand for quite some time where your finances are concerned. It's time for you to pull your head out and start breathing fresh air again. Once you make a buck or two—or even *save* a buck or two—you will begin to grow more and more excited about the impact your own personal decisions can make on your financial future.

The keys are to take charge, to start now, and to be consistent. I'm reminded of the instructions on your shampoo bottle (the ones no one ever bothers to read): "Lather, rinse, repeat." Only, in our case, it goes a little something like this: "Set a goal, reach it, set a new goal." It is my hope that this mantra—Set a goal, reach it, set a new goal—becomes such an ingrained habit that you won't need to give it any conscious thought anymore, that it will just be there, under the surface, every day of your life.

2

Knowing Where You Are Is Half the Battle

(A Self-Analysis)

Have you ever started a diet? Have you ever looked at yourself in the mirror after the holidays, tried to button a pair of pants, or stood winded at the top of a flight of stairs and said to yourself, "It's time for me to get in shape?"

What's the first thing you should do before committing to a diet or fitness program? You should step on a scale. You may not want to read what that scale has to say, but how else can you gauge your results if you have nothing to compare them with? Furthermore, numbers don't lie.

In this sense, budgeting your money—losing that debt, firming up your bottom line, and getting into good financial shape—is no different from losing weight, toning up, or slimming down. You'll never know how much weight you've lost if you don't step on the scale right at the beginning.

As unpleasant as it may be to face reality, there's no better time than the present to kick off your shoes, take a deep breath, step on that scale, and see how much you and your current debt load actually weigh. (You never know; you might even be pleasantly surprised!)

Today is the day you step on that scale, with me beside you. (Think of me as your personal finance trainer.) This is the day you drag out your old checkbooks, dust off those unopened bank statements, sort through your receipts, and find out what kind of financial shape you're really in.

There will be no smoke and mirrors, no excuses about allowing five pounds for your running shoes or sports bra. These are real numbers we're talking about, and we need them to be accurate in order to gauge your future success.

Don't worry; regardless of the state of your finances, you're far from alone. In my line of work, I've seen budgets that come in all shapes and sizes—from those that barely allow for a weekly meal at a fast-food restaurant to those that take into

13

account a spouse's $15,000 monthly shopping allowance. However much weight (debt) you're packing, chances are I've known people with more. Whatever grandiose dreams keep you tossing and turning at night, I can help you make them real.

There is no budget too small or dream too big to shock me anymore. I sat down to write this book because I got tired of seeing people spinning their wheels and thinking they could never, ever get themselves into good financial shape again. I know better, and now you will too.

Here is my one and only secret: you *can* save money, invest, and grow wealthy if you really want to. All that's required is an intense commitment to facing the challenging road ahead and a sensible plan for navigating it.

What Is Your Endgame?

I always tell my clients that arranging their personal finances is a lot like writing a mystery novel: you have to know "whodunit" before you begin writing page one! Whether your ultimate goal is to get out of debt, to save money, or to make good investments—or a combination of all three—you must target your endgame before you even get started on your path toward your ultimate goals.

You must ask yourself honestly and seriously: what is your ultimate goal? What are you trying to get out of this process? Why are you reading this book? Why are you willing to make sacrifices? Do you intend to save more or to spend more efficiently? To give up or sacrifice? To rework or to discard? Until you answer these questions for yourself, honestly and with clarity, there's really not much that I—or anyone else, for that matter—can do for you.

My clients all have different goals and dreams. Some of these are realistic given their current earning potential or debt load, some less so. Regardless, I frequently hear the same aspirations:

"I want a new house."
"I want to quit work and go back to school."
"I need a new car."
"I'd like to go on vacation this year."
"I wish we could send our child to the best college possible."
"I want to start putting money away for the kids."

Sometimes the dreams are a little far-fetched for a person's current financial situation. It's hard, for example, to invest in stocks and bonds when you're still getting troubling calls from collection agencies because of bounced checks and maxed-out credit cards. But debt—no matter how big—*can* be managed. Progress *can* be made, money *can* be saved, and you *can* begin—right now, today—the process of investing in your own personal financial future.

The first thing I'll suggest to you is the first thing I suggest to each and every client who sits at my desk: putting yourself in your own personal financial driver's seat means knowing where you want to go before you get in the car.

You wouldn't think of taking a road trip without a final destination in mind, would you? Knowing where you're going helps you plan for the journey. It helps you budget for gas, pack the cooler, pick out the roadmaps, and put air in the tires.

Keeping this in mind, why do you think you can start investing money before you've settled your debt? Or save for your child's college fund if you have to bounce a check to buy them shoes?

Setting unrealistic financial goals is like trying to drive from Los Angeles to New York on half a tank of gas. You just can't get to your final destination without proper planning, and the first thing you must plan for is where you want to go in the first place.

Understand Your Spending

(Understand Yourself)

Most people have no idea how much money they spend every day. It's human nature to rationalize spending, mostly because it's not just our finances, but also our emotions, that come into play. After all, spending money often makes us feel good.

Whether we're buying a new CD or a hamburger, a silk tie or a pair of shoes, we experience a pleasant chemical rush whenever we put down our hard-earned money and get something—anything—in return.

"Individuals will get some kind of high from an addictive behavior like shopping," says Ruth Engs, a professor of applied health science at Indiana University. "Meaning that endorphins and dopamine, naturally occurring opiate receptor sites in the brain, get switched on, and the person feels good, and if it feels good they are more likely to do it—it's reinforced."

So, you see, it's not our fault that we like to spend money. Not only does our enjoyment of spending have a biological root, but we also live in a society of consumers governed by politicians who spend money to solve problems and are surrounded by advertising-saturated media that constantly tell us to "buy, buy, buy." Even city planners contribute to this dilemma: ads at busy intersections beckon us to purchase a multitude of products. Restaurants feature drive-through windows that make it easier for them to hawk coffee, pastries, burgers, and fries. Department stores have everything we need under one roof, and half-price sales urge us to "spend more to save more."

Too often, we're too busy "saving money" to analyze how buying two rolls of paper towels for $2.84 saves us more than a couple of pennies as opposed to buying one roll for $1.41. The come-on sounds so appealing—the half-logic seems so whole—that it *must* be saving us money, right? But department stores, advertisers, and chain coffee shops spend millions of dollars a year on advertising that takes advantage of the fact that you're usually too busy to notice that "deals," in the end, cost you money, not save you money.

Logic often goes out the window when you're hungry and food is in front of you. Budgets fall and financial planners' warnings are forgotten when the scent of grilling meat combined with an enticing opportunity to "buy four tacos and get one free" overpowers them. You forget that you could make a taco at home for seventy-five cents. Instead, you buy one at the intersection for $1.50, thereby "saving" yourself a valuable ten minutes in the kitchen back home. Okay, it may cost twice as much, but it takes only half as long. And besides, it's *only* a dollar-fifty!

In the grand scheme of things, a dollar fifty isn't terribly important. (Nor, for that matter, is it the beginning of a great financial plan). But you'd be amazed by how those small amounts can add up after a week, a month, or a year of fast-food tacos, movie tickets, and new CDs. I'm not trying to send you on a guilt trip regarding your spending habits. I simply want to make you aware of them. This is something that all good financial planners should do.

As I say to my clients, "Understand your spending; understand yourself."

I never suggest that my clients go "cold turkey." Habits are hard to change, and any lasting habit must be hard-won over a period of constant change. But we *must* change if we are to save more, spend less, and have a secure financial future. What I *do* suggest to my clients—and strongly, at that—is that they at least begin to understand their spending so that they can realize the huge amount of waste that occurs in our country—and in their personal checking accounts—every single day.

I'm not suggesting that we shouldn't enjoy ourselves, treat ourselves, or even indulge ourselves. After all, what's the point of working hard and getting paid if we don't enjoy ourselves a little along the way? It's the constant trickle of easily overlooked small amounts of wasted money that I try to point out to clients in my early consultations with them. Financial analysts call this process "leaking money," and we Americans do a lot of it.

Let's examine our moviegoing habit. The average theater ticket costs about eight bucks these days. A bag of popcorn costs around three dollars. A soda? Add another two bucks. Throw in a box of candy, and we're talking two more dollars. So, what is the costs of a night out for two? Twenty-three dollars.

This is hardly extravagant, by any means, but still a lot more expensive than renting a movie to watch at home for three or four dollars and making a healthy dinner in the kitchen. A night out at the movies is a simple expenditure, really, and is for most people a totally harmless one. It becomes a problem, however, if you're sitting across from me complaining that you can't afford to make the eighty-dollar monthly payment on your credit-card debt. How am I going to help you find this money? I'm going to look at the so-called "little things" you regularly buy.

Do you and your spouse go out to see a movie once a week? Why, there's ninety-two dollars per month right there. ($23.00 per week x 4 weeks = $92.00.) You can't hold a movie, touch it, drive it home, or wear it to work. And yet, it costs nearly a hundred dollars a month. In a year, that's about $1100 down the drain, with nothing tangible to show for it.

Just so that Hollywood doesn't get mad at me, let me stress that I'm *not* saying that you shouldn't go to the movies. What I *am* saying is that *if* you're looking for somewhere to start curbing your spending, always look for the "little things" first. Rent, electricity bills, and car payments are all big expenditures that you can ill afford to let slide. But morning coffees on the run? Movie night with all the trimmings? Dinner out three, four, even five times a week? Drive-throughs, vending machines, cigarettes, lighters, an extra beer or glass of wine at last call? *These* are the little things that can add up to big savings if you can begin, week by week, to cut them out.

Debt Is a 4-Letter Word:

Handling Emotional Spending with My Emotional Debt Reduction System

I have suggested that you understand your spending habits in order to curb them. I also urge clients to curb spending habits so that they can free up money that can be used for other things. The most important of these "other things" is getting out of debt.

The majority of my clients who are in debt have gotten themselves there by using their plastic a little too often. Credit-card debt is by far one of the most insidious and costly detractors from family and individual budgets today. It's so easy to accumulate, and it's so hard to eliminate.

Or is it?

As a matter of fact, it *is*.

But I have a simple strategy that works well for my clients, and I'll share it here with you. No matter how many credit cards you have, no debt load is impossible to carry if you begin the process of reducing it right now—*today*. It can *seem* insurmountable, I know, when you're staring at three, five, or maybe even fifteen thousand or more dollars in debt owing on your credit cards.

But you can learn to curb your impulse to charge your purchases, and even pay off your credit cards one at a time, systematically. First, you must understand your spending. Second, you must start using my Emotional Debt Reduction System by paying off the credit card with the lowest limit first.

Huh? Aren't you supposed to pay off the card with the *highest* balance first? Technically, that would be great. But emotionally, my way works better. Why? Simply because people want to see an accomplishment. They want to feel good, particularly about their debt.

Credit cards, plastic, revolving accounts ... they all carry emotional weight from the minute we open them. We know that we should only buy what we can afford to pay for with cash, but the temptations to open a revolving account or "just charge it" are so strong—and everybody else is doing it—that quite often they're simply too hard to resist.

So, right off the bat, we associate credit cards with feelings of guilt and, all too often, regret. "I really didn't need that," we say, "but it was right there at the counter, and I was charging everything else anyway, so ..." How many of us experience a "credit hangover" in January as a result of the shopping excesses we charged during the holiday season in December?

Instead of trying to make my clients feel worse about an already grim situation, I try to give them some hope—and, in the process, change their behavior—by introducing to them a way to manage debt.

Notice that I didn't say "eliminate debt." Why not? Isn't it my job to get rid of your debt? Well, yes and no. Yes, it would be great for you to get rid of *most* of your debt, but I would not suggest that you get rid of it all. Just as some stress can be positive—the kind that makes you perform at your professional peak when you're striving to meet a looming deadline, for instance—I believe that some kinds of debt are actually good.

Take your house. It's probably not only your biggest asset, but your biggest tax write-off as well. So why would you want to pay it off? Our preconceived notions about debt—that we should have none, carry none, want none—sometimes get in the way of the opportunities presented to us by modern lenders. By keeping mortgages on our homes, we are able to utilize, leverage, and master these opportunities, thereby enabling us to afford such expenditures as our children's education, occasional expensive emergencies, or even improvements to make our homes more attractive.

Likewise, managing credit-card debt is a much more realistic pursuit than eliminating it. If I were to tell my clients to eliminate their credit-card debt, I would have a lot of cancelled appointments in the following months. Not only would they not be able to do it, but the embarrassment they would feel at their failure would also make them not want to face me.

Instead, we work together to manage their debt so that as they pay off their cards one at a time, their confidence grows, their spending habits tighten, and, best of all, the positive experience of managing versus eliminating their debt begins to affect their very behavior.

So, unlike most financial planners, I look at my clients emotionally first, and financially second. Hence, my Emotional Debt Reduction System of paying off the credit card with the lowest limit first.

Think of your credit-card debt as a pyramid. You don't want to start at the bottom—where the base is wide and the debt is dense—and work your way up. No, you want to start at the top—where the debt is much smaller and easier to handle—and work your way down.

Trust me, the benefits really start to snowball if you can pay off, for example, a credit card with a $500 balance first, then add the amount you had been paying to that first card to the payments for the second card, which has, say, a $1,000 balance on it. Before long, you will find yourself paying off *all* of your cards faster.

Keep in mind that while the interest rates of your credit cards are important, the amount of true debt—the balance owing on each of your cards–is *more* important.

Let's say that you're carrying balances on three credit cards at the moment. One card carries a debt of $1,500 at 19 percent, another carries a debt of $1,000 at 15 percent, and a third carries a debt of $3,000 at 20 percent. Which one do you pay down first? That's right: the second one. What? You didn't say the second one? You said the third one?

Wrong.

It's true that the third one has a higher interest rate, and therefore you might think, "pay it first, because it's costing me the most." Mathematically, you'd be right. But emotionally, you'd be wrong.

It might seem smarter, on paper, for you to try to pay down the card with the highest debt and the highest interest rate. But this is not the smarter choice if you *never actually do it!* You have to be realistic—not just with me or with your own financial planner—but with yourself. It does you no good to sit in my office and make me dramatic promises when you're *still* going to stop on the way home and charge purchases to that high-balance, high-interest card!

This is why I'm a much bigger fan of goals than I am of budgets. A goal can be reshaped, revisited, and rewritten. A budget can only be one thing: broken. So, we are emotional so we get emotional. We own our emotion, face it, and even call it my Emotional Debt Reduction System.

Let's say you did try to pay off Card #3—the one with the $3,000 balance at 20 percent. Your minimum payment is $35. You and I agree that to pay it off in a timely manner, you need to not just double that amount but actually quadruple it to $140 a month. You skip movies for a month, as well as your morning take-out on the way to work, and you make that first payment of $140. Let's say that you even make your second payment of that same amount, and your third, and your fourth. (Congratulations!)

But five months without movies or coffee does not a happy camper make. The credit-card bill has now taken on a whole big emotional life of its own. You dread its arrival in the mail, you dread writing that check, and you really, *really* want to see a darn movie! So, the fifth month, you only send in $125. That's all you can afford. And, since you "broke your budget" that month, the next month you send in even less, and the next month even less, until once again you're back to sending in the minimum and are no closer to paying off that biggest card than you were when you started.

Now consider what would happen if you were to use my Emotional Debt Reduction System and pay off the credit card with the lowest limit first. This means that you attack the one with the $1,000 balance first. The current minimum payment is $25. Forget that. We really want you to feel good about vaulting over this first debt hurdle, so you promise yourself to send in a whopping $150 per month.

At first, this requires a huge adjustment. You don't just skip the movies and morning coffee drinks, you even miss a concert or two, go without that new DVD you'd been planning to order from Amazon.com, and maybe even forego season tickets to your home team. (Now, *that's* dedication!) You send in that first big check, and then another, and another. It feels good—scratch that, it feels *great*—to see the balance go down by $150, then $300, then $450! You haven't just attacked that balance, you've practically demolished it, and nearly half of it has disappeared!

Month four arrives, and it's really hard to send in that $150. You're sorely tempted to blow it all on movies, CDs, basketball tickets, and a brand-new cell phone. You spend a few rough days wavering, but then you get your latest statement in the mail, see that new, low balance, and think of how nice it would be to get it under the $500 mark. And with your latest payment, you can do just that. So you keep your promise to yourself, write the check, and send it off.

Three months later, you're rewarded when the card is finally at a zero balance and you can move on to the next account. Eureka! Simply by choosing the right card—the one with the lowest balance—you've turned failure into success. You've started at the top of the debt pyramid, where it's easier, and have begun to work your way down, instead of starting at the bottom (with the high-balance, high-interest card) and only making it up a few feet before sliding back down again.

It may not be smarter by the book to start with the smallest card, but I that think by now you'd agree that it's smarter for *you* to start with the smallest card. This is because by paying off the smaller balance first you have *achieved a goal,* which will provide you with incredible motivation to achieve your *next* goal. You are ready to tackle the next card.

I would suggest that you pay the minimum plus ten dollars to all of your cards, then focus on paying double—if not triple even quadruple—the monthly payment to that smallest card until you pay it off. Once it has been paid off, you should take it out of your wallet or purse and *leave it at home.* Just flat-out act like you don't have it, and chances are that you won't use it. Then take the amount you had been paying on that smallest card and add it to the minimum payment of the next card. Card by card, that debt pyramid is going to get smaller and smaller. With each card you pay down or off, you'll have that minimum balance plus whatever you're currently paying on the others to pay down the rest.

I know that it's hard to imagine taking a credit card out of your purse or wallet. You've become used to just taking it out and not paying for lunch with cash. I suggest that you use your bank debit card instead of your credit card. Most of these now carry the VISA or Master Card logo, the money will be paid directly from your account, and you won't have any big interest charges at the end of the month, nor will you add any new debt to your current load. Remember that your goal is to get out of debt, and that if you keep adding debt, you will never accomplish your goal!

Perhaps now you can see why I insist that you understand your spending before you try to get out of debt. By spending less—be it at the movies, the coffee shop, the mall, or the record store—you will have more money available to pay down your credit cards. Cut out going to the movies every week, and you free up nearly a hundred dollars to pay down—or pay off—your smallest credit card.

Often, clients will come in carrying a huge credit-card debt and want to "start investing" right off the bat. They get frustrated when I tell them they won't have anything to invest until they pay off their credit cards.

To them, it seems like I'm putting the cart before the horse.

To me, it's like paying for the horse before you buy the cart!

In their minds, investing is the only means of attaining a bright financial future. They're partly right: investing *is* important to your economic well-being. However, once they realize that lowering expenses will gradually free up money that they can later invest, they get a little more excited about paying down their debt.

Now, what happens when you've finally paid off your third and final credit card? That's right—it means that you're ahead of the game because you don't have to send the credit-card companies any more money. It means that you've freed up capital to invest.

Saving money *is* making money.

It just doesn't feel like it at first.

Sign a Contract

(With Yourself)

Sure, it may *sound* easy for you to give up your weekly movie fix, but what happens when that new *Star Wars* or *Matrix* movie comes out and you just can't *not* see it? My simple response is: "Go see it!" An eight dollar movie ticket is not going to make or break your finances, but now is not the time to sit back and count your piles of money.

By being more mindful of your expenditures, you will no doubt learn to save some money when you *do* go to the movies—by going earlier in the day to take advantage of matinee rates, buying a smaller bag of popcorn, or skipping the candy. This doesn't sound as though it would save much, but, as we've already seen, a little often means a lot.

At the end of the day, it's a commitment issue. What, specifically, are you willing to commit to? What goals can you set for yourself that are easily defined, comfortably attained, and realistic?

Unlike most financial planners, I don't really believe in budgets. To me, putting a client on a budget is just courting disaster. Budgets don't say something positive, like "you can," but rather something negative, like "you can't." And your budget doesn't just chide you once, but every time you take out your wallet, write a check, or whip out the plastic.

You can't buy this. You can't afford that.

For most people, finances already prompt negative emotions. Some of this is drummed into us in our youth, when our allowance is never enough to buy the toys we really want or the junk food we surely don't need but really want anyway. Later, we experience more negativity when our friends at school—our peers—always seem to have more money than we do. Later still, this negativity is reinforced when we're faced—or when our parents are faced—with the exorbitant costs of college.

Once we hit the so-called "real world," we find out for ourselves just how rarely our finances make us feel positive. So, as a financial planner, I believe that an important part of my job is to make the financial aspect of a client's life a positive one. I want to make them feel good about money again—like they did before they realized that their allowance would never stretch as far as they thought it might. Do you remember how good it felt to stick pennies into a piggy bank and count them out each month? Do you remember how good it felt when Aunt Clara sent you that whopping ten-dollar bill for your birthday?

That's the feeling I want to engender in my clients, and in you. Budgets, I've found, don't produce that feeling. In fact, budgets produce quite the opposite feeling. Sometimes, the damage a bad budget can do overpowers almost anything else a good financial planner might achieve.

On the other hand, I do believe—quite strongly—in setting goals. Many people consider the two are equal in stature, but, in fact, they are as different as going on a crash diet and living healthy for a lifetime. A budget is temporary; it's short-term. Your goals, on the other hand, are links in a chain that goes on forever. Once a goal is reached, the first thing you do is make a new goal. Therefore, reaching a goal produces a positive feeling, whereas failing to keep a budget results in a negative one.

This is where a contract will come in handy. A contract, although it sounds severe at first, is really nothing more than a goal crystallized. Once a client commits to a goal such as opening an IRA or paying off a credit card, I like to gauge their level of commitment by having them sign a contract—not with me, but with themselves.

Since it's written down on paper, the simple contract takes on the appearance of a real and binding one. I've discovered that if a person performs the symbolic act of signing a document that says, for instance, "I, John Doe, commit to saving $100 a week for the rest of the year," he will, in fact, follow through on his promise. I suppose it's just human nature to treat a signed, official-looking document more seriously than a handshake and lip service. Whatever the reason, I can tell you—non-scientifically, but with absolute certainty—that my clients who do sign a contract with themselves perform better, as a group, than those clients who don't sign one.

The best thing about a contract with yourself is that it does *not* represent a budget; it represents a goal. Yes, the contract might accomplish the exact same thing—it might save you money, devote money to investments, slow your spending, or whatever—but when we commit to a reachable goal and put it to paper, it blows a budget straight out of the water.

Your contract doesn't require you to hire a notary, buy an expensive pen, have witnesses, or store it in a fireproof box. A simple piece of paper and a ballpoint pen will work just fine. What's important is that you sign the contract and stick to it.

The more specific you are in your contract, the better. For instance, a contract that states, "I, John Doe, commit to saving $100 a week by cutting out movies, fast food, cappuccino, and new CDs" is much more effective than one that leaves out the specific ways in which you intend to save money.

And don't just sign your contract—"publish" it. By this I mean that you should put it where you can see it all day, every day. Use it as the wallpaper on your computer monitor. Tape it to your fridge. Better yet, make a dozen copies of it and paste them everywhere you spend time during the course of your day—at home, at the office, and even in the car.

Another tactic that works quite well is to use your contract as a guide and, once you've committed to an amount, instruct your bank to automatically deduct that amount from your checking account at specified times and place it wherever you're directing those funds, such as a savings account, a college fund for your kids, or a credit-card payment.

Many people might complain that they could never do something like save $400 a month. But look at the luxuries that make up our sample list: movies, fast food, cappuccinos, and new CDs. I didn't say food, entertainment, dinners out, or anything else that a normal person can't live without. (And if you *know* that you can't live without splurging on a new CD every week or going to the movies, don't put it on the list. Choose something else that you *can* live without, but something that costs about the same.)

Between signing the contract with yourself and arranging for direct deposits with your bank, you are taking firm, logical, rational, money-saving steps *today*. You aren't just making empty promises or procrastinating, you're doing something positive that will effect your future, and sooner than you think!

Many of my clients say "I can't afford $400 a month. There's just no way. Forget it." But then I set up a direct deposit for them, and a few months later they come in and say, "Has that started yet?" Meanwhile, $400 has been siphoned out of one account and into another, and they haven't even missed it. When you don't see the money in your hands—when it's not burning a hole in your wallet—it's much easier to let it go.

On the other hand, if I were to ask my clients to come to my office with $400 at the end of each month and let me deposit it for them, I'm sure that I'd have a few dozen cancelled appointments on the last day of each month! Human nature makes it very difficult for us to physically save a five-dollar bill here or a twenty there, stuffing them under our mattresses or folding them into secret compartments of our billfolds. If you do things my way, however, the money will be gone before it ever reaches your hands. It literally becomes unavailable for non-necessities.

Sometimes, in other words, to make a little "money magic" happen, we have to trick ourselves.

Sarah's Story

(Sound Familiar?)

Sarah came to me two years ago, highly distressed. She was engaged to be married, and she had what she considered a dirty little secret: she was $18,000 in debt. She had five maxed-out credit cards and was desperate not to saddle her husband-to-be with what she considered her "foolish spending habits."

Sarah was an intelligent woman who was successful in every other aspect of her life—she had a great job and a great relationship with a great fiancé. But her not-so-great finances were a heavy weight on her shoulders. Sarah was living proof that the traditional way of paying off debt doesn't work for most people. She confessed that she'd tried to pay down her debt on her own by doing just what I typically advise against: paying off the highest-interest, highest-debt card first before moving on to the smaller cards with smaller debts. Like most of my clients who try this technique, Sarah failed. She so rebelled against the unpleas-antness of always having to pay so much toward the biggest card that she simply stuck her head in the sand and ratcheted up the balances on *all* her cards!

This is a very common reaction, and a prime example of how people respond emotionally to debt instead of logically. In fact, people almost always approach their finances from an emotional, versus a rational, frame of mind. It's kind of like dieting: you tell me that I can't eat this or can't eat that, and my head nods in agreement and understanding, but my stomach rebels. It says "no" in many ways throughout the first week of any diet. It says "no" when it rumbles late at night. It says "no" when I reach for the sugar-free cookies instead of the apples. It says "no" when I go to the fast-food restaurant instead of the gym.

That's why "budget" is a bad word in my office. If I tried to put people on a budget, they would immediately start to think about cheating on it. It's not their fault. It's simply human nature. To deny ourselves is to invite temptation. We always want what we can't have, be it a triple-decker cheeseburger with curly fries or a purchase that we can't afford but charge anyway.

My role is to help clients experience how good it feels to pay down debt. I can't simply steer them toward their goal with spreadsheets, graphs, pie charts, and balanced checkbooks. They've got to feel a real desire for the goal, deep down, where their emotions rule their pocketbooks, bank accounts, and credit cards.

Sarah was clearly emotional about her financial state of affairs. She'd read many self-help finance books, taken all the free financial quizzes on the web, and talked to relatives who advised her well. Sarah knew exactly what to do. She just couldn't make herself do it.

Sarah didn't want me to hide her debt; she wanted me to help her get rid of it before she got married. (Fortunately for us, she had a long engagement!) With no time to waste, we got right to work. I shared with Sarah my emotional debt phi-losophy that she should pay down the card with the lowest balance first, and we set about finding out how much she could afford to devote to that card each and every month.

At first, she balked. "Aren't I supposed to pay the highest balance off first?" she asked. "I mean, that's what all the books I've read said to do."

I quickly explained to her my budget/diet philosophy of emotional saving. I told her that when my clients pay off their smallest credit card first, they immedi-ately feel a strong sense of satisfaction. They feel proud of their accomplishment and are thus more dedicated to paying off the next-biggest credit card, and then the next, and so on.

People always try to separate their finances from their feelings, but I've learned that the two are actually quite intertwined. Just think of how we describe many things related to spending with emotional terms. Many people say that they actually feel "high" when shopping. Retailers call the day after Thanksgiving "Black Friday" because their ledgers finally come out of the red. And Realtors call the tens of thousands of dollars their clients spend to secure a house the "down payment."

As I always say, knowledge is power. So, when we know that we tend to get emotional about our finances, we're much more able to deal with it. When I gave Sarah "permission" to pay down her smallest credit card first, I could see a wave of relief wash across her face. Frankly, she couldn't wait to get started!

And start we did. When we studied Sarah's spending habits, she quickly realized (as do most people) how much money she could free up simply by cutting out life's little extravagances. She was particularly embarrassed to realize, after sifting through some particularly coffee-stained receipts, that she literally spent twenty dollars a day on iced cappuccino!

Systematically, by using my "emotional debt formula" of paying down her lowest card first, then her next lowest, and so on, Sarah was eventually able to meet her realistic financial goal. By the time she started planning the wedding, her credit-card debt was within reach of being completely wiped out. While paying down her credit cards, she soon caught what I call "financial fever."

She became addicted to saving money or, in lieu of that, spending wisely. She had driven to our first consultation in an overpriced SUV she neither needed nor could afford. A month later, she'd traded it in for a sporty compact car with much better gas mileage and a far lower monthly payment.

This two-for-one savings step—spending less money on gas *and* on car payments—allowed her to put even *more* toward her credit cards each month than we had planned. She paid off the first one that much more quickly, and she was then able to pay off her other cards more quickly as well. Her early steps initiated a kind of reverse snowball effect—just as a snowball grows as it rolls down a slope, Sarah's debt seemed to shrink at a comparable rate.

She soon became what I call "financially savvy." She invested in *Quicken*, consulted it every day to see where she stood with her spending, saving, investing, and so on, and was able to enjoy her wedding with a clean conscience and with a much-improved credit rating!

Recently, Sarah sent me a thank-you card to express her gratitude for my having taught her what she already knew: that leaking money is the quickest way to get yourself in hot water!

Don't Just Change Your Bank Account

(Change Your Habits)

I should call this "Sarah's Story, Part 2," because it also stars our favorite newly-wed. When Sarah first came to my office, she also came clean: "Finance," she said to me that fateful day, "is scary to me!"

Many of my clients share this sentiment. Before that day, Sarah had rarely even opened her financial statements, let alone studied them. I opened a half-dozen of her dusty bank statements that were still sealed in their original envelopes and had been tucked away in her bureau drawer.

I found this especially odd because Sarah was so good at her job, which, amazingly enough, revolved around balancing her employer's accounts. What she could do for others, she simply couldn't do for herself.

Sarah didn't so much balance her checkbook as "guesstimate" it. In other words, she spent what she *thought* she had and charged the rest! I considered her very lucky to have never bounced a check. Credit intuition or just plain luck, Sarah had managed to live a lifetime in the financial dark, but her panic-stricken face during our first consultation suggested to me that you could hardly call it "living."

I'll never forget how Sarah's far-reaching goals didn't reflect her reality, and how they mirrored the expectations of so many of my other clients. She wanted me to invest what little money she did have left over each month—after only paying the minimum on her $18,000 of credit-card debt—and use the return to pay off the cards. She came to my office that day not to save money but to make it so that she could get out of debt.

I quickly set her straight. Even if I could get her a 22 percent rate of return on a given investment—which is excellent by anyone's standards—these profits would only equal the unheard-of 22-percent interest rate she was paying on her five credit cards! Even if I had made Sarah good money during those two years of her long engagement, it wouldn't have made a dent in her debt. Slowly, with a few solid examples, I was able to show her—as I hope I've been able to show you—that saving money really *is* like making money. In Sarah's case, it was even better!

What Sarah learned over the course of her "reversal of debt" was not just to change the figures in her bank account, but to change her very habits. Anyone can see the absurdity of spending twenty dollars a day on iced coffee, but it takes a real habit change to save that money instead.

The best thing about Sarah's story is that it had the happiest possible ending. Once she met her goal, she didn't go back to buying four iced cappuccinos every day. Her new good habits simply wouldn't allow it. Sarah didn't just undergo a reversal of fortune during those two frugal years—she actually *changed*. She caught financial fever and keeps it burning to this day. Sarah changed her life not by paying off $18,000 in credit-card debt; she changed her life by correcting the very habits that got her into debt in the first place.

Money comes and goes. Good habits are forever. Good habits make good money better and stretch any amount of money farther. Good habits help you take care when you're making a lot of money and take even greater care when you're not.

Good habits last through the holidays and birthdays, through good times and bad. Like marriage itself, they last "in sickness and in health." By the time you're done with this book, I want you to be armed with more than just facts and figures, formulas and plans. I want you to have learned how healthy it is to develop good spending, saving, and investing habits that will last long after you close this book.

I want your habits to be good so that your life can be even better.

You'll Never Cross the Finish Line …

… If You Don't Picture Yourself Breaking Through!

As we end our chapter on fresh beginnings, I want to leave you with one final message: don't start something you can't finish. If you're setting yourself up for failure, why start the journey in the first place? Don't assume that you need to invest money right away. It may take longer, but settling your debt first will make things better in the long run.

Sarah came to me full of wild hopes and dreams of making it big in the stock market, paying off her debt, and maybe even paying for her honeymoon as a bonus. I could have indulged her fantasy and gone through the motions. My retainer would have been the same. But I wanted to teach Sarah good habits that would last her a lifetime.

I can't stress enough the fact that Sarah had a firm, clear, definable goal to help her stay the course when things got tough, days got long, and she really, *really* wanted that fourth cappuccino of the workday! The final elimination of her $18,000 in credit-card debt was the goal that Sarah fought so hard to reach. She chipped away at it day by day, saving by saving, statement by statement, until she broke the $17,000 mark, then the $16,000 mark, and so on.

When your goals are clearly defined, they're simply easier to reach. So don't analyze your spending, pore over your bank statements, and then say to yourself, "I want to make a million dollars next year." For most people, this is not a realistic goal. You would be setting your finish line too far off in the distance. The goal would be so far away that you might not even see the starting line, let alone the finish!

Maybe paying off $18,000 of debt represents too distant a finish line for you to cross. The dollar figures are not the important part of Sarah's story. What *is* important is that she set a realistic goal, put an action plan in place, took steps to achieve it, and stuck to her guns. I would have been just as proud of her for paying off $8,000 or $800—as long as she'd stuck to her plan.

As we end our chapter—and begin our journey toward your financial freedom—keep in mind the fact that Sarah's final outcome was more successful than it could have been, but was not as rare as it might sound. Every single day, new people join that fabled 5 Percent Club. Some join after receiving an inheritance, and others join after winning the lottery, but the vast majority of them join as a result of sheer hard work, setting clear goals, and having one heck of a financial plan.

It's not easy, but it's worth it. Don't let the story of your finances be a mystery. Know how it ends before you start writing it, and write a new chapter of it every day.

3

First Things First (Managing Debt)

"When I want a bigger house, I first buy assets that will generate the cash flow to pay for the house."
—Robert T. Kiyosaki author of *Rich Dad, Poor Dad*

Leverage.

I want you to think about that word for a minute: leverage. Really, really think about it. *Leverage. Merriam-Webster Dictionary* defines it in its financial sense as "the use of credit to enhance one's speculative capacity." And that's how we'll be using the word, too.

But synonyms of the word "leverage" in its other senses include such terms as "force," "power," and "control." Forget leverage for a minute and think of those other three words.

Force.

Power.

Control.

They're not words you often hear to describe your monetary potential, are they? But why not? Why do we concentrate on the negative instead of the positive? Why do we see the bank account as half empty rather than half full?

This book is about changing not just the positions of the decimal points in your financial ledger, but the very way you feel about money. It's about changing your emotions as well as your spending habits, your feelings as well as your finances. This all starts with the very way you think about money.

Wouldn't it be nice to see money as a thing of *force*, instead of feeling forced into spending it, feeling that you're not making enough of it, or feeling a profound sense of weakness?

Wouldn't you like to feel more powerful when it comes to your money? Wouldn't you like to feel the *power* of earning real capital, gaining real assets, and amassing true wealth?

And, lastly, wouldn't you like more *control* over your own finances? And not just control over the money you need today to pay your bills or buy your groceries, but over the money you'll need in the longer term, for your retirement?

Leverage.

Leverage is what can give you that force, that power, and that control. But leverage isn't just a dictionary term, a financial buzzword, or an entry in my thesaurus.

Leverage is a financial philosophy I stumbled upon early in my career, one that has enhanced my life in numerous ways ever since, and a concept that you need to become very, *very* familiar with if this book is to do more than just occupy another slot on your bookshelf.

Speaking of which, how many of the other financial books on that shelf have you really read? Some of them are great, sure. In my case, some of them are well-thumbed, dog-eared, highlighted, and not on my shelf at all but on my desk, my nightstand, or even in the backseat of my car, ready for me to read during those notorious LA traffic jams. But most of them are worthless. Why? Because they don't help you change your emotions. They don't address the emotional aspect of spending, buying, borrowing, or paying down.

They might have told you *how*, but they didn't show you *why*. Guilt doesn't work. Fear doesn't work. Humor doesn't work. Facts don't work. Figures, colors, graphics, and charts don't work, either. Only one thing will work for you, for me, for all of us: behavior modification. We have to do what we say we're going to do and spend the way we know we should spend in order to save the way we know we must.

It's not about denying yourself—about budgeting or spreadsheets or ledgers or calculators—but about becoming wiser in the way you manage your money—in particular (for this chapter), in how you manage your debt. None of those books, classes, seminars, stock tips, e-mail leads, pithy quotes, fancy tickler files, and daily planners amount to a hill of beans if you had to stretch your finances to pay for them all! Your behavior, not your lack of knowledge, is at the root of your problem.

Remember: leverage isn't just a way to increase wealth, but also a way to manage debt.

Leverage represents a way of thinking about every aspect of your finances, from how you make simple daily buying decisions to how you handle life's big-ticket items, like education or retirement. This chapter is about debt. More specifically, we'll talk about how to leverage what you have to pay off what you owe!

When a House Is Not a Home

(But Is More Than a Home)

Robert T. Kiyosaki, author of *Rich Dad, Poor Dad* and about a dozen other bestsellers, is one of my favorite writers, and I'd like to share one of his sayings with you: the way to tell if something's an asset or a liability is to note whether it puts money into—or takes money out of—your pocket.

I love this definition because, much like leverage, it gives you real power. In this case, it's the power to apply the definition—money into or money out of your pocket—to anything you buy, own, rent, or sell. In this section, we are going to focus on applying that definition to what is for most people their biggest (potential) asset: the family home.

As author John Malz states in a recent article from *Real Estate Weekly*, "America is in love with real estate! 67% of American families now own their own home, a 50% increase since 1950. Well, why not? It's a bonafide tax shelter, with mortgage interest and real estate taxes a deduction against income, and liberal forbearance against payment of capital gains tax. Now add to the economics the ever present importance of having a stable home and roots in a community, it would appear that the wisdom of investing in a single family home is unassailable."

Or is it? Given Kiyosaki's definition, a home typically takes money out of our pockets every month, rather than putting money back in. Unless you've paid off your mortgage, your house is really an asset for your bank, not for you. After all, you're paying them every month.

Technically speaking, then, your home is a liability. But we're focusing on emotion, not technicalities, in this book. In the last chapter, I suggested that your home could be a great asset to you in the future, not by paying it off, but by using it as a tax shelter, a debt-manager, or an income-generator, among other things. But how? How do you turn this liability into an asset?

The only way to make your house an asset is to leverage the borrowing capability to which it entitles you. That's right, in this chapter about "managing debt" I am suggesting, of all things, borrowing. More specifically, I'm suggesting that you do exactly what a bank does: borrow money at a lower rate to "sell" at a higher rate. Even *more* specifically, I'm suggesting that you take money out of your property at a lower rate and put it into a fixed annuity or bond—or one of the many other products we'll talk about in later chapters—that pays a higher rate than your mortgage, and thereby gives you more equity.

It's really important at this part of your journey to stop and consider the fact that the equity in your home may very well be the most money you can ever make outside of your primary income. Looking at your earning potential realistically, an equity shift in your property appraisal of even 5 percent could quite possibly beat the best raise you've ever had.

Let's say that you're sitting on a $250,000 house and property values in your neighborhood rise an average of 5 percent. This would mean that your house is now worth $262,500—a jump of $12,500! If you were to get a raise like that next year, it would truly be something to write home about.

This kind of profit doesn't have to exist only on paper. You can *leverage* your home equity—not just to put in a pool or build an addition—but to literally create income with which you can pay down your mortgage debt.

If this sounds a little like robbing Peter to pay Paul ... well, it is, and it isn't.

Let me explain why.

"But I Thought You Said We Were Managing Debt!"

When is borrowing different from going into debt?

When you're borrowing for all the right reasons!

Just like some debt is good, as I told you in the last chapter, *managing* debt is sometimes better than being debt-free—particularly when you own your own home.

In this case, whereas by dipping into your home equity you're creating more debt on the mortgage side, you're also leveraging that debt with a higher return. This higher return makes your assets more manageable.

Make no mistake: no investment is risk-free. However, by reinvesting your home equity in low-risk or fixed-return investment products (which we'll soon discuss), you can pay yourself rather than the bank. The strategy may sound unusual, but it's really a simple one. I predict that once you've tried it, you'll become a firm believer, just like myself and many of my clients.

When I first give my clients advice that seems to fly in the face of most of the advice they've ever been given regarding home equity loans, I can usually see the doubt in their eyes.

Most of us take out a second mortgage in order to reinvest the money into our houses. To a certain extent, this makes sense. Putting in a new pool for $18,000 might add another $25,000—on paper—to the value of your house. This isn't a *bad* investment, by any stretch of the imagination. But when you apply our asset-liability definition, you'll realize that it creates a liability on top of a liability—you're now paying the bank a mortgage on your house, *and* you're paying your contractor a fat monthly check for the pool, all the while hoping, but far from certain, that you'll get all that money back one day.

Using my strategy of investing your equity, on the other hand, you'll actually be paying down your mortgage more quickly because the rate of your investment return will pay a higher return than your cost of borrowing the money in the first place. You'll literally be turning a liability into an asset.

And that, my friends, is what debt management is all about.

New Meaning for the "Home Office"

Most financial advisers say that you should pay off your home. This can be good or bad, depending on how you want to live. If your home is your largest write-off, for instance, paying it off will eliminate your ability to write off that income. In other words, by following advice that's not tailored to your own situation you may be making a move that's not right for you.

When you've finished reading this book, I want you to feel confident about your finances. I want you in control of your money or, barring that, in control of your emotions as they apply to your money. This means listening to any financial adviser with both ears open—use one to collect good advice that applies to you and the other to filter out generic advice that, much like a horoscope or a fortune cookie, could apply to just about anybody.

I've talked a lot so far about spending habits. More has been said about the first part of that phrase—spending—than has been said about the second part—habits. It's time for me to rectify that.

Your house says a lot about how you spend money. In other words, your house reflects your habits. Can you afford your house? Was it below your budget, right at your budget, or more than you could really afford? What about the contents of your house? Do you pay for your furniture and appliances in installments, or do you save up until you can afford to pay the full amount? Do you charge the contents of an entire room all at once, or do you buy it piece by piece, with cash? Do you open a revolving account at a department store to buy brand-new dishes, silverware, pots, pans, and other kitchen accessories every year or so? Do you own flashy gym equipment that you never use—equipment you may have bought over the phone during late-night infomercials you were only watching because you were so far in debt that you couldn't sleep?

Keep in mind I'm making no judgments about any of the above behaviors. (Okay, maybe about that last one, but that's it!) That's a good word, though:

"behaviors." It reflects the fact that these types of purchases are manifestations of how we feel, think, and act around money.

Why? Mainly because these emotions—these habits—often reflect poorly on your finances. Most of my clients spend more than they earn. They don't do this because they're extravagant, out of control, or have a death wish. Most of them are very successful professionally but not so talented financially, even though many of them make large amounts of money.

I tell them that it's not how much they make but how much they spend that's most important. And they often spend more than they make simply because they can. Everything can be bought over time these days—houses, cars, pools, gas, fast food, movies, CDs, clothes, big-ticket appliances—you name it, you can charge it.

Think about it: a new credit card with a credit limit of just $12,000 can allow you to spend $1,000 more than you earn in any given month. Two credit cards with that same limit means you have access to an extra $2,000 a month. Three cards? That's an extra three grand!

You can see how a typical client of mine who makes $5,000 a month can easily spend $7,000 a month. None of my clients are bad people—or foolish people, for that matter. They simply don't pay close attention to what they spend. The money comes, the money goes, and as long as the checkbook balances at month's end, everything's fine. We quickly get into a habit of knowing *roughly* how much money there is in our checking accounts, and when we get close to depleting it, what do we do? Stop spending? Heck, no! We just whip out our credit cards and charge the overage.

We feel no pressing need to curb our spending habits, to change our behaviors, or to go without the things we want. (Notice that I didn't say *the things we need*.)

Very few of us could walk into our boss's office and ask for a $2,000 monthly raise. So how can we earn that extra money? Furthermore, how can we earn the extra money that will allow us to pay down the debt we've accumulated because we've stopped saying "no" to ourselves?

To earn income you never thought you had, I want you to stop treating your house like a mere residence. Instead, treat your house like a company. You wouldn't overextend a home business, would you? Why give yourself permission to do the same with your house? If you're bringing in $5,000 a month but spending $7,000—$2,000 of it on credit cards—your "business" has a bad debt ratio, thanks to even worse spending habits.

If you can't cut out the $2,000, you have to find a way of generating income. This is where income-generating investment comes in. If you own a home, you can use your home equity to leverage enough generated income to actually help you manage your debt more efficiently.

Keep in mind that sometimes your best investment choice is to pay off your credit cards. Consider that the national average balance on a single credit card is $9,000 and that the average interest rate is 18.75 percent. It is very difficult—if not impossible—to generate a monthly return that can compete with these numbers. (I'm good, but not *that* good!)

"But Cory, borrowing money to pay down debt!" I can hear you saying. "Is that really a good idea?" Well, the short answer is: only if it works for *you*. Only if you're comfortable with the concept, the risk, and the opportunity. If you're not comfortable, then the answer is *no*.

The long answer is a tad more complicated.

Have you ever bought someone a gift and tried to take off the price tag, only to have half of the price tag come off, leaving a sticky white mess behind? Well, a friend once showed me that if you take the half of the price tag that *did* come off, curl it around your finger or fold it over so that the sticky part is on the outside, and apply it to the half of the tag that's still stuck to the gift, it will actually begin to pull the residue off. Slowly, by repeatedly applying the sticky side of the removed portion, you can remove the entire original tag. Pass after pass, sticky rip after sticky rip, the old tag will come off. Eventually, you will find that you've solved the problem.

This is very similar to what I've been talking about regarding your finances. You'll be taking some money out of your equity (using the sticky side of the price tag) to make a better return, so that you can pay down your original debt (the ugly, left-over piece of the price tag).

A lot of people only withdraw money from their home's equity to fix it up. What is the resulting profit ratio? Where is the payoff? How can you spend that money if you need it? Most importantly, how can you use that money to create a rosier financial picture for yourself? If you take out the money and invest it, on the other hand, you'll be making money on that money immediately instead of putting it back into the house and hoping to collect on it at some indeterminate time in the future.

I'm not suggesting philosophies without having some proof that they work. I use the "home equity solution" myself. For me, it wasn't just a case of thinking outside the box—it was more a case of listening to my heart. As anyone will tell you, the real estate market in California—and particularly Los Angeles—is out and out crazy at the moment. What sells for $300,000 elsewhere sells for twice that much out here, if not more. The situation was even worse two years ago, when I bought my dream house for $720,000.

Everybody told me to wait—that the bubble would burst, the market would bottom out, and the trends would reverse. But I didn't listen. I knew that I needed to apply sound financial principles not just to my business but to my personal life as well. I knew that this purchase in particular would provide me with not just the building, the property, the tax shelter, the write-off, and the equity, but, most importantly, with the *opportunity* to practice what I'd been preaching all my professional life.

So I bought the house when the market was high not just because I knew it would be a smart move, but also because it was the emotionally correct choice for me to make. I felt in my gut that it was the right thing to do. I firmly believe that we should plan smart to act smarter. By acting I mean physically acting—taking advantage of an opportunity because, in plain English, it "just feels right." I believe in sticking with emotional commitments when they're that important.

My house quickly became an income generator. While the markets elsewhere wavered—while the real-estate bubble never quite burst, but slowly, steadily, and sadly deflated—the LA housing market remained strong. With the equity on the house rising each year, I could borrow against the house to pay down the mortgage. I borrowed intelligently to pay down debt by generating income from the equity.

Today my house is worth $920,000 on paper, but its true value has been appraised at $1.4 million because of various upgrades—custom cabinetry, surround-sound stereo in all rooms, a pool, and more—and its equity has increased even more each year as I've paid the mortgage down.

I accomplished this not through secret connections or insider knowledge, but by treating my home like a business.

It was my biggest liability at one point, and my goal was to make it an asset instead!

Applying Leverage in Your Own Personal Way

Leverage.

I started this chapter with that word, and I want to end it on the same note because leverage is the one driving force in debt management. If you utilize what you have, you open yourself up to a world of new opportunities. You have to become enthusiastic about your finances, or my lessons are all for naught. You have to believe that you can generate income, manage your debt, and free yourself financially, or you'll never truly be at ease with your own money.

I want you to think of a number: $100,000. It seems big, doesn't it? Many people strive to save that much in a lifetime and never get there. After all, there are only so many days in a week, dollars in a paycheck, and pennies left over at the end of a year. To save $100,000 in any traditional manner takes know-how, time, and lots and lots of sacrifice. And I've already explained to you how hard it is for us to deal with sacrifice.

But just look at what has happened in real estate over the past few years. Everyone I know—from doctors to lawyers to actors to cashiers to busboys to bag boys—seems to have a story about how they "made it big in real estate." Many of these stories are even true. The fact is that many people who bought a house in 2001 and, by the time 2005 rolled around, had at least—*at least*—$100,000 in equity on that very same house.

They might never have been able to save that much the old-fashioned way, but they earned that much simply by investing wisely. In this case, they invested wisely in the real-estate market. But what is that money doing there if it's not being used wisely? What good is $100,000 in equity if you don't make use of it? (Remember that most millionaires earn their original fortunes in real estate, but *increase* their wealth by investing in the securities markets, i.e. stocks and bonds.)

You have to think of that money as capital. It's waiting there for you to put it to good use. I hope that this chapter has shown you *why* that money can be used to pay down debt, earn income, and leverage your liability into an asset.

In just a little while, I'll show you *how*.

4

Identifying Your Profit Personality

What *is* a "profit personality," anyway? Simply put, everyone has a personality—not just when it comes to their home life, family, friends, or workplace, but when it comes to their bank accounts as well.

When you go to a public function—a cocktail party, for example—isn't there a certain side of your personality that people are used to seeing? You might be the fun, flirty "life of the party" who people can't wait to be around. Or you might be the wallflower type, who stands back and observes the scene while waiting for the best possible opportunity to join a conversation. I hope you're not the stuffy bore, the know-it-all, or the lampshade-on-the-head guy. You might certainly be the dutiful hostess. These are all personalities we've seen at almost every cocktail party we've ever been to.

Why should investing be any different? We all have "profit personalities," and I see a variety of them every day. They may not wear cocktail dresses or lampshades on their heads, but they are clearly identifiable nonetheless.

I can sit across from a new client and in five to ten minutes know his or her "profit personality." I can predict how he'll react to my suggestion to invest in a mutual fund or how she'll become upset if I suggest that she invest more aggressively.

I'm no mind reader. I simply make observations that I've learned to interpret after nearly two decades in the financial sector. My "trick" is a little different—and often less glamorous—than that of the waitress who knows all of her regular customers. She knows what they like to eat and drink, how long they'll sit at their tables, and what they'll tip her when they finally leave. Over the years, the products, the markets, and Wall Street itself might have changed, but the profit personalities pretty much stay the same.

Why does this matter? Money's money, right? Well, yes and no. I always tell my clients that knowledge is power, and while money *is* money—$100 is $100 no matter how you slice it—the most valuable asset in investing your money is your *knowledge of yourself.* This is a message you've heard before in this book, but now you're finally going to come face to face with the most important person in your investment future: *you.*

In my years as a financial advisor, I have identified six basic profit personalities. I've listed each and described each of them below, and you will have to determine which of them sounds most like you. Fair warning: people tend to see a little bit of themselves in each of the descriptions. The truth is that there is no *absolute* profit personality. My six are merely gatherings of traits that tend to associate with one another. Investors are typically either aggressive *or* reluctant, deadly serious *or* happy-go-lucky.

The point of this chapter is to get you to learn a little more about who you are, so that in the next chapter—in which we'll begin to discuss the various products on the market today—you'll be able to base your decisions on what you've learned about yourself.

Profit Personality Type 1:

The Maverick

The Maverick enjoys the thrill of seeking financial gain. He sees his investment portfolio the same way others might view an amusement park brochure. There is often no rhyme or reason to his so-called "strategies."

Be it real estate or the latest Wall Street stock offering, the Maverick buys and sells at the drop of a hat. He bases his investments on mood swings or some internal whim that makes him act on snippets of financial information, whether they be from legitimate sources or mere hearsay. The Maverick might have heard his latest stock tip from a reliable financial source or from the guy in front of him on line at Starbucks. This latter strategy is a good one only if the guy in Starbucks is Warren Buffet; to the Maverick, it doesn't matter if it was Warren Buffet, Warren Beatty, or Jimmy Buffet—once he gets a "hot stock tip," it's nearly impossible to dissuade him from acting on it.

Performance is irrelevant to the Maverick. He lumps good tips together with bad ones, and rarely bothers to study the performance of any of them. The Maverick forgets about the tips that make him money as soon as he forgets about the ones that cost him. He might as well be playing with Monopoly money!

The financial Maverick typically engages in the following practices:

- He subscribes to several investment newsletters or other publications (although whether he reads them or just arranges them on his coffee table remains unknown

- He stays informed about current products on the market

- He eavesdrops on financial conversations whenever he can, no matter who is speaking

- He keeps an eye out for the next get-rich-quick stock

- There is no structure or pattern to his buying or selling

- He tries out every investment available, from options to real estate

- He listens to no one but himself

- He simply *must* be in charge, and second to none

Profit Personality Type 2:

The Professor

Meet the Professor. This cautious type of investor is typically quite smart and may even have an engineering degree or similar background. He is a lifelong student, a lover of learning, and a firm believer not only that is knowledge power, but that one can never have too much knowledge. He approaches investing the same way he approaches everything else in life: cautiously, studiously, and analytically.

As a result, he often overanalyzes things. He turns them over in his mind and doesn't act on them until he has repeatedly studied them from every possible angle. As one might imagine, he usually ends up taking too long to react to information he receives. Therefore, he often misses out great investment opportunities.

The Professor prompts the question: how much knowledge is too much knowledge? In other words, when is it time to study, and when is it time to react? I am a great proponent of research; in the financial sector, doing one's homework can often mean the difference between success and failure. But there is such a thing as too much of it

As you might imagine, the Professor:

- Reads a lot of information

- Subscribes to several investment newsletters and other publications (and reads them all cover-to-cover)

- Avoids making financial decisions until he believes that he has a complete understanding of the situation

- Takes a long to time to make a decision

- Is often too cautious to make any move at all

Profit Personality Type 3:

The Pessimist

Say hello to the Pessimist. This type of investor is typically negative, always fears the worst, and knows that she *should* invest but will list a thousand reasons not to. The Pessimist will complain when she is not making money and make blanket statements like, "Why does this always happen to me? I bet everybody else is making money in this market!" She will also complain when she *is* making money. Her profits are never enough; she should be making *more*. When things are going the Pessimist's way, she still sees her glass as half-empty. When she's losing money, on the other hand, she complains that, "I knew I shouldn't have bought that product! Why am I so stupid?"

The Pessimist:

- Waits to see what happens

- Avoids making financial decisions for as long as possible

- Needs to be reassured constantly

- Will worry about a problem later instead of taking action to fix it today

Profit Personality Type 4:

The Shrinking Violet

This type of investor is typically quite gun-shy about parting with any of her assets and must be thoroughly coached before making any type of significant—or even comparably insignificant—investment. She seems to be taking part in a constant struggle—every decision is weighed and weighed again, then taken off the emotional scale, and then weighed some more after the scale has been reset.

Does this sound familiar? Unlike the Professor, however, the Shrinking Violet doesn't use facts, research, and analysis to evaluate her decisions. Instead, she troubles over them all in her mind.

You would think that everyone who came into my office was ready to commit. Not the Shrinking Violet. If I had to give her a psychological diagnosis, I would choose a well-worn cliché and say that she had some serious "commitment issues."

The Shrinking Violet:

- Has a hard time balancing her checkbook

- Spends without investigation—sometimes too much, sometimes too little

- Avoids making financial decisions as long as possible

- Can't be bothered with discussing finances in detail

- Never opens her statements

Profit Personality Type 5:

The Conservative Investor

The Conservative Investor typically does things that could be considered "normal:" he saves a little, owns a few stocks, is aware of how much equity is in his home, and may or may not own a computer program like *Quicken* or *Money*, but he basically deals with his finances only when it's convenient.

I call this the "default setting" for the majority of my clients. Most Americans, in fact, tend to think like Conservative Investors. It's only when my clients and I get to know each other better and start hashing things out that other profit personalities show themselves. If any of the others don't appear, then I know that I'm dealing with a Conservative Investor.

The Conservative Investor …

- Can get quite excited about a particular investment opportunity but balks at committing to it

- Reads one or two books on finance per year, but rarely acts on their advice

- Has good intentions but poor follow-through

- Thinks about doing things "someday"

- Usually keeps the bulk of his assets in banks

- Wants big gains but doesn't want to take the risks necessary to achieve them

Profit Personality Type 6:

The Investor (My Favorite)

The Investor is simply my favorite type of client to work with. She takes her money seriously and knows that in today's tough economic times she must take her finances as seriously as she does her health, work, and social life. In other words, our appointments are not an afterthought, duty, or nuisance. She is educated enough to understand the basic rules of personal finance, but not so presumptuous as to assume she knows everything.

She has done her homework on different types of investments and is fully prepared to move forward each time we meet. While she could most likely make her own investment decisions and do just fine, she seeks out professionals to help her make sound decisions.

The best thing about the Investor is that she can be a little like all the other profit personality types when she has to be—she can be a Shrinking Violet when a situation demands it, or she can be a Maverick. She changes her behavior to do what she knows is best for her bottom line.

Sometimes, her Maverick instincts pay off with a big win because she took risks. When they don't, she carefully records the failure and uses additional research to make the loss into a gain by learning from it.

Conversely, if her Shrinking Violet tendencies cause her to miss out on an opportunity, she doesn't blame herself (like the Pessimist would) or blame me (like the Professor might). Instead, she sighs, blinks twice, and vows to weigh her options more carefully and proceed more decisively next time.

The Investor:

- Regularly watches CNBC or some other financial news network

- Subscribes to two or three investment newsletters or other publications

- Owns a diversified portfolio

- Understands her personal spending habits and knows how to manage debt

- Makes decisions based on long-term objectives

- Has a great family and work life

- Has some form of spiritual balance

Perhaps, like most of my clients, you have a little bit of each of these types of personalities. You may think you're a Maverick, but find yourself nodding your head at the Shrinking Violet. Don't worry—this is perfectly natural. Quite often, how we act is the polar opposite of how we feel. Don't you know people who are actually quite shy on the inside but who outwardly play the role of the aggressive boss, breezy socialite, or popular jokester?

I'm no psychiatrist, but, in my office, people's actions often reveal that they are quite the opposite of who they say they are. We can mask our thoughts or talk a good game, but, when it comes down to signing a check, withdrawing a certain amount, or making a firm investment, we usually show our true colors. I often see the true Shrinking Violet on the inside warring with her outward Maverick when it's time for her to sign on the dotted line. I see the reverse just as often!

No matter how many profit personalities you think you have hiding inside yourself, there is one lesson I want you to take away from this chapter: *know yourself.* Understand who you are.

Facts, figures, books, charts, journals, Web sites, stock quotes—these are all tools for making decisions, not the decisions themselves. I firmly believe that people will do what they *want* to do, not what someone *tells* them to do. At the end of the day, they will do what best reflects their nature. If at heart you are a Maverick, then trying to change your style of investing will be difficult, to say the least. If you are a Maverick, then *be* a Maverick. Embrace it, live it, learn it, enjoy it, use it!

Instead of trying to be more like another profit personality type, accentuate what you're good at. Focus on your strengths instead of obsessing about your weaknesses. Not only will you learn more about yourself, you will also learn how to make sounder financial decisions.

5

Products, Strategies, and How They Work

We've finally arrived at my favorite section of the book! In fact, I could write an entire book just about products and strategies alone—that's how valuable I think they are. Unfortunately, there are too many products and strategies to describe them all, so I have chosen some of my favorites for you and will explain how you can best make use of them.

First, let's clear up a few common misconceptions. When most people ask me about investing, they almost certainly have only two things in mind: stocks and bonds. This is how their parents invested their money, it's what they grew up hearing, and they think that stocks and bonds are all that's available to them on today's market.

But there are *many* types of investments available today. Limiting your investment strategy to just stocks and bonds is a little like walking out your front door wearing only your underwear. Sure, they'll cover the basics, but there are a lot of items of clothing out there that will cover you a lot better. I don't say this to knock stocks and bonds—they're still valuable means of making steady money in an uncertain time—but to educate you about the alternatives.

Before I continue, I'd like to say a word about my definitions. The word "investing" is so loosely used today that it can refer to almost anything—mutual funds, real estate, or absolutely any other product that can generate a return on your money. All of the products I'll be talking about are "investments." Investing, after all, is merely the act of committing money to earn a profit. The products I will be discussing are the means of creating that profit.

Investing 101

Beginning at the Beginning

I call this section "Investing 101" because learning to invest—particularly learning about various products and strategies—really *is* an education.

I recognize that all of you will be coming at this information from various stages of the learning process. To some of you, the following information may look like it's written in another language! To others, it will be old hat. Most of you probably have at least some familiarity with the names of the products and some of the terms I'll be using. But, like many of my clients, you may need a quick refresher course before you seriously begin the investment process.

Where should we begin?

Since mutual funds have been preoccupying a lot of my clients lately, I've chosen to talk about them first.

What Is a Mutual Fund?

A mutual fund is a pooled investment. When you buy shares in a mutual fund, you are buying shares in a professionally managed portfolio of various stocks, bonds, or other securities. Mutual fund managers are responsible for buying and selling the securities that comprise the fund according to specific investment objectives.

What Types of Mutual Funds Are Available?

There are thousands of different mutual funds on the market. They range from funds that include a broad variety of investments to funds that invest exclusively in single securities or narrow sectors of the market.

Since there are many different investment styles and objectives, there are bound to be a number of mutual funds that are suited to your personal investment profile. Every fund has its own expense, risk, and return characteristics. Be sure that you understand these characteristics before you invest. There are fifteen principal types of funds. I have listed growth, income, and specialized funds according to their primary objectives.

Balanced Funds

Balanced funds seek to obtain the highest return consistent with a low-risk strategy. They hold a mix of common and preferred stocks, bonds, and cash reserves. The combination can vary according to current market conditions. Balanced funds may offer higher yields than pure stock funds. Balanced funds are generally the least risky of the growth-oriented mutual funds.

Growth and Income Funds

Growth and income funds attempt to achieve both long-term growth and current income. They invest primarily in high-yield common stock, preferred stock, and convertible debt (bonds) to generate both growth potential and current income. Because they include a mix of investments, these funds are typically less risky than growth funds.

Growth Funds

Growth funds seek long-term appreciation by investing in the stocks of established companies that may be poised for growth. These companies typically pay low dividends yet offer the potential for long-term capital appreciation. Some growth funds limit their investments to specific sectors of the economy. Growth funds are generally less risky than aggressive growth funds.

International and Global Growth Funds

International and global mutual funds offer diversification into international stock markets. International funds invest only in foreign securities. Global funds, on the other hand, can invest in both foreign and U.S. securities. The risks associated with investing in foreign products include differences in regulation of financial data and reporting, currency exchange differences, and the uncertainties that may surround economic and political systems that differ from those of the United States.

Aggressive Growth Funds

Aggressive growth funds, sometimes known as "small-cap" funds, seek maximum capital gains. They invest primarily in the stock of smaller, less established companies. Since these companies generally pay out small or no dividends, aggressive growth funds rely on capital growth for returns. These funds tend to be the riskiest of growth-oriented mutual funds.

Money Market Funds

Money market funds seek current income while maintaining a stable $1.00 per share net asset value by investing in short-term debt securities including T-bills, certificates of deposit, commercial paper, and other highly liquid and very safe securities. They offer modest current income and no potential for capital gains. They generally offer the lowest returns but the most safety of all fund types. Some money market funds also offer tax-free income. Money market funds are neither insured nor guaranteed by the Federal Deposit Insurance Corporation or any other government agency. Although such funds seek to preserve the value of your investment at $1.00 a share, it is possible to lose money by investing in the fund.

Government Securities Funds

Government securities funds invest primarily in Treasury and government agency securities. Because they are issued or guaranteed by the U.S. government, they are considered the creditworthiest alternatives available. Government securities offer moderate current income and high safety. Treasury securities are backed by the full faith and credit of the U.S. government, which guarantees timely payment of principal and interest. Government agency securities, on the other hand, are *not* considered government obligations and therefore are not backed by the full faith and credit of the government. The principal value of these funds fluctuates with changes in interest rates.

Municipal Bond Funds

Municipal bond funds seek tax-free income by investing in the bonds of state and local governments. In many cases, it may be wise to consider municipal bond funds issued by your own state because they may offer double or even triple tax-free income. In some states, you will have to pay income tax if you buy shares of a municipal bond fund that invests in bonds issued by other states. In addition, while some municipal bonds in a fund might not be subject to regular income taxes, they might be subject to federal, state, or local alternative minimum taxes. If you sell a tax-free bond fund at a profit, there are also capital gains taxes to consider. As with all types of bond funds, the principal value will fluctuate with changes in interest rates.

Corporate Bond Funds

Corporate bond funds invest in debt securities issued by corporations. The risk of corporate bond funds varies depending on the objectives of the fund. Because credit risk is somewhat higher, these funds may offer higher returns than funds specializing in government securities. Principal will fluctuate with changes in interest rates.

High-Yield Bond Funds

High-yield bond funds seek to maximize current income by investing in lower-quality, high-yielding corporate bonds. The bonds held by these funds are generally rated BB or lower by rating agencies. They offer high current yields to compensate for their greater risk of default. Since they are more volatile and pay higher yields than investment-grade bonds, they tend to be suited to investors with high risk tolerance.

International Bond Funds

International fixed-income funds invest in debt securities of foreign governments and corporations and seek to provide current income. Global bond funds may include U.S. government and corporate bonds. The risks associated with investing in foreign products include differences in regulation of financial data and reporting, currency exchange differences, and the uncertainties that may surround economic and political systems that differ from those of the United States.

Other Types of Funds

Aside from growth and income funds, there are a variety of mutual funds that limit their investments to a particular sector, index, or other specialized criterion. Depending on your investment objectives and tolerance for risk, these funds might be considered additions to a portfolio containing more traditional types of funds.

Index Funds

Index funds are mutual funds that attempt to match the performance of a particular market index. For example, a stock index fund may hold stocks that mirror the performance of the S&P 500 or the Dow Jones Industrial Average. Index funds provide broad diversification within a single type of asset class.

Precious Metals Funds

Precious metals funds invest directly in precious metals or in the stocks of companies that mine them. Most of these funds limit their investments to gold and gold bullion or to shares in gold-mining companies. The returns from precious metals funds come primarily from long-term capital appreciation.

Asset Allocation Funds

Asset allocation funds are those that give their managers great flexibility in deciding how to invest fund assets. A fund manager can invest in any of the major investment classes, including stocks, bonds, and money market securities. The weighting of each class may vary dramatically and will reflect the market outlook and expectations of the fund manager.

Sector Funds

Sector funds invest in specific industries or sectors of the economy, such as communications, aerospace and defense, or health care. While they may be diversified within a particular sector, they lack broad diversification. This increases their investment risk. These funds typically seek long-term capital appreciation.

Socially Conscious Funds

Socially conscious funds invest exclusively in the securities of socially conscious companies. For example, this type of fund may not invest in companies that cause environmental pollution or that have interests in countries with repressive governments.

The value of mutual-fund shares fluctuates with market conditions. When they are sold, these shares may be worth more or less than their original costs. Bond funds are subject to inflation, interest rates, and the credit risks associated with the underlying bonds in the fund.

Benefits of Mutual Funds

As you can see, there are many types of mutual fund on the market. Why is this important? Well, throughout the book, we have talked about having choices, and being able to pick a well-allocated mutual fund can mean the difference between retiring in ten years and retiring in twenty.

Mutual funds are popular investment vehicles simply because they offer a wide variety of features to suit the objectives of many types of investor. These features include built-in diversification, professional management, convenience, low investment minimums, and a wealth of investment choices—all in one package.

Diversification

Buying shares of a mutual fund gives you built-in diversification. A single mutual fund holds many different securities. Mutual funds may diversify within asset classes. For example, a growth fund may invest in a portfolio of stocks. Alternatively, a fund may diversify *across* asset classes—a balanced mutual fund can invests in both stocks and bonds, for instance. Whatever the case, diversification generally reduces investment risk and provides the potential for better long-term returns.

Professional Management

When you buy into a mutual fund, investment professionals manage your money. They carefully research, select, and supervise all of the assets in the fund. This frees you from having to select and track individual investments. When you invest in mutual funds, you get access to some of the finest investment minds on Wall Street.

You should remember, however, that past performance is no guarantee of future results. The value of your shares will fluctuate with changes in market conditions, and, when they are sold, your shares may be worth either more or less than the original investment amount.

Flexibility

Often, mutual funds belong to a "mutual fund family." You may be able to shift your investment among different types of mutual funds, often with no more than a phone call. This makes it easier for your portfolio to be tailored to suit your financial situation and your expectations about the market.

Convenience

Mutual funds make managing your portfolio very easy. Periodic statements will advise you of the performance of your mutual fund, transactions within your account, and more. You'll also be kept informed about the tax consequences of your distributions.

Low Investment Minimum

Finally, many mutual funds offer low minimum initial investment amounts. Some can even be below $1,000. The value of mutual fund shares fluctuates with market conditions. When sold, shares may be worth more or less than their original cost.

Before You Invest in Mutual Funds

In short, mutual funds offer a wide variety of benefits. They can be ideal investment vehicles for experienced and beginning investors alike. Mutual funds are sold only by prospectus. Please consider the investment's objectives, risks, charges, and expenses carefully before you invest. A company's prospectus, which contains this and other information, can be obtained from your financial professional. Be sure to read the prospectus carefully before deciding whether to invest.

Variable and Fixed Annuities

The next products that I would like to talk about are variable and fixed annuities. I realize that there are a lot of misconceptions about annuities. Most of my clients believe at first that after money is put into an annuity, it cannot be recovered. They also think that annuities are unwise investments. Personally, I believe that annuities can be some of the *best* investment vehicles today, if we can only learn to use them the right way.

And, of course, you must learn which is the right type of annuity for *you*.

What Is a Fixed Annuity?

An annuity is a contract between you and an insurance company. In exchange for a current premium, your insurer agrees to pay you a minimum fixed rate of return and a future stream of income. Fixed annuities are very flexible financial vehicles. You can pay your premium all at once, or you can pay it over time—it's up to you. In addition, you can specify when you would like to begin receiving the income from your annuity. You can start immediately, or you can let your annuity accumulate.

One of the most attractive features of fixed annuities is that they are allowed to grow with the taxes on them deferred. Because you do not have to pay taxes on annuity growth until it is withdrawn, annuities have become an attractive accumulation alternative.

Immediate Fixed Annuities

With an immediate annuity, payments usually begin one month after you have paid a lump-sum premium. This makes them popular sources of supplementary income for retirees.

Immediate annuities provide some tax deferral. Only the interest portion of each payment is considered taxable income. The rest of the payment is considered a return of your principal. Taxes on the earnings of the annuity are spread over the payout period, which means that you pay less in taxes in the early years.

Deferred Fixed Annuities

With a deferred annuity, you allow your premiums to accumulate before you begin the payout period. Deferred annuities give you the option of paying fixed or flexible premiums, and you can pay them all at once or over time. The earnings on the annuity are not taxed until they are withdrawn. This may allow you to accumulate more over the long term than would taxable investments. And *you* decide when to start receiving income from this type of annuity.

Annuities are insurance-based financial vehicles designed to provide income in retirement. There may be a 10 percent penalty on amounts withdrawn prior to age 59½, in addition to regular income taxes. Surrender charges may also apply in the early years of the policy. There are also fees and expenses to consider. The guarantees of a fixed annuity are contingent on the claims-paying ability of the issuing company.

What Is a Variable Annuity?

A variable annuity is one that provides variable rather than fixed returns. The key feature of a variable annuity is that you have control over how your premiums are invested.

When you pay your premium, you choose from a variety of different investment "subaccounts," which include stock, bond, and fixed-interest options. Your premium can be distributed among these portfolios. Unlike fixed annuities, which pay fixed interest, the value of your variable annuity is based on the performance of the subaccounts you select. These subaccounts will fluctuate in value and may end up being worth more or less than their original cost when redeemed.

A Tax Strategy

Variable annuities provide the dual advantages of investment flexibility and the potential for lower current taxes. The taxes on all interest, dividends, and capital gains are deferred until withdrawals are made.

When you decide to receive income from your annuity, you can choose a lump sum, a fixed payout, or a variable payout. The earnings on the annuity will be subject to ordinary income taxes when you begin receiving your income.

A Host of Other Benefits

Variable annuities offer a host of benefits. They are suitable for using investment strategies such as asset allocation and dollar cost averaging. Variable annuities are flexible, and they can be tailored to suit the needs and objectives of just about any investor. Insurance companies offer a variety of services designed to make this financial strategy easy to implement and maintain.

What Control Will a Variable Annuity Give Me?

Fixed annuities combine preservation of principal, fixed returns, and tax-deferred growth. This makes them a unique alternative to other taxable accumulation vehicles. But what about investors who want more control over their annuities? What about investors who may be seeking greater long-term growth potential than that offered by fixed annuities?

Fortunately, you have a choice. Variable annuities combine the tax-deferral benefits of fixed annuities with investment flexibility. This makes variable annuities a popular alternative for many types of investors.

Considerations

As with other types of annuities, you should be aware of surrender charges and the 10 percent penalty for withdrawals prior to age 59½. Variable annuities are sold only by prospectus. Please consider the investment objectives, risks, charges, and expenses carefully before investing. The prospectus, which contains this and other information about the investment company, can be obtained from your financial professional. Be sure to read the prospectus carefully before deciding whether to invest.

Insurance as Investment:

When Peace of Mind Helps You Get a Piece of the Investment Pie

Now that we have talked about mutual funds and annuities, I'd like to introduce the different forms of insurance you may need for your peace of mind. Let's start with life insurance. Many people think that insurance acts contrary to, or in addition to, their investment strategy.

I believe that insurance is an *investment*—it's an investment in your future, because it means money for your family after you're gone. Some of the insurance policies we'll talk about in this chapter can even act like savings accounts for times of need. I wouldn't go so far as to suggest that you invest *all* your money in insurance, but you definitely shouldn't ignore the possibilities of insurance when you're rounding out your portfolio!

The first type of life insurance we can talk about is "term life." Term life insurance is "pure" insurance. When you purchase a term policy, you are buying coverage for a specific period of time. If you die within the time period specified in your policy, the insurance company will pay your beneficiaries the face value of your policy.

Term Insurance

Term insurance offers temporary protection. This differs from the permanent forms of life insurance, such as "whole life," "universal life," and "variable universal life," which generally offer lifetime protection. And, unlike other types of life insurance, term insurance accumulates no cash value. You don't receive a refund at the end of the policy period if you haven't died. Term life insurance may be appropriate for temporary life-insurance needs or when your cash requirements make permanent life insurance unaffordable.

Term insurance is sold for a specified period of time. Annual renewable term life insurance is renewable every year and does not require proof of insurability. Its main drawback—one that also affects other types of term insurance—is that premiums increase every time you renew your life insurance coverage. The reason for this is simple: as you get older, your chances of dying increase. As the likelihood of your death increases, the risk that the insurance company will have to pay a death benefit increases as well. Unfortunately, term insurance can become too expensive when you need it most—that is, in your later years.

There are several variations on term insurance that allow for level premiums. For example, you may be able to obtain five-, ten-, twenty-, or even thirty-year level term, or level term payable to age sixty-five. You can also buy decreasing term life insurance, for which you pay level premiums for a death benefit that decreases every year. Each of these types of term life insurance has its own particular uses. For example, decreasing term insurance is often used to provide the funds to pay off a home mortgage if a spouse dies.

Whole Life Insurance

Most people are familiar with whole life insurance. For many years, whole life was the predominant type of life insurance sold in America. When you purchase a whole life policy, you traditionally pay a fixed premium for as long as you live or for as long as you keep the policy in force. In exchange for this premium, the insurance company promises to pay a set benefit upon your death.

In addition to providing a death benefit, whole life policies build cash value.

Part of your premium goes to the insurance company to pay for the pure protection element of your policy. The remainder is invested in the company's general investment portfolio. The insurance company will pay a guaranteed rate of return on the portion of your policy that is in the investment portfolio.

This cash-value buildup is part of the reason why the premiums on a whole life policy generally remain fixed for the duration of the policy instead of increasing to match the increased risk of death. As the cash value of your policy grows, the risk to the insurance company declines. Your stake represents an increasing share of the face value of the policy.

Although the cash value of your policy is "your" money, you can't simply withdraw it as needed, as you would with a savings account. You *do* have access to your funds, though.

To withdraw these funds, you can either surrender the policy for its cash value or withdraw the needed funds as a "policy loan." Outstanding loans, however, will reduce the policy's death benefit. Be aware that in addition to charging you a modest interest rate for borrowing the funds, the insurance company may pay a lower rate of return on that portion of your cash value that represents the amount you borrowed. Policy loans are generally not taxable and can provide the cash to help with unexpected expenses.

The cash value of a life insurance policy accumulates tax-deferred. If you surrender the policy, you'll incur an income tax liability at that time, but only for those funds that exceed the total amount of the premiums you have paid.

One of the attributes that makes whole life policies so attractive to some people is troubling to others. This is the fixed premium and fixed death benefit. To some, this means one less thing to worry about. They know in advance what they'll have to pay in premiums and exactly what their death benefit will be. For others, this doesn't provide enough flexibility. If their situation changes, they will likely be unable to increase or decrease either their premiums or death benefit on their whole life policy without being forced to surrender it and purchase a new policy.

Still, the level premium and fixed death benefit make whole life insurance very attractive to some.

Universal Life

Universal life policies offer a great deal of flexibility. Universal life insurance was developed in the late 1970s to overcome some of the disadvantages of term and whole life insurance. As with other types of life insurance, you pay regular premiums to your insurance company. In exchange for these premiums, the insurance company will pay a specific benefit to your heirs upon your death. And, as with whole life insurance, a portion of each premium goes to the insurance company to pay for the pure cost of insurance. The remainder is invested in the company's general investment portfolio.

Most universal life policies pay at least a minimum guaranteed rate of return. Any returns above the guaranteed minimum will vary with the performance of the insurance company's portfolio.

You won't be able to exercise any control over where these funds are invested. The insurance company's professional portfolio managers will manage them. But there *is* an area where universal life policies offer a great deal of control.

Universal life policies are very flexible. As the policy owner, you can vary the frequency and amount of the premium payments. You can also increase or decrease the amount of the insurance payout to suit changes in your situation. If your financial situation improves significantly, you can increase your premiums and build up the cash value more rapidly. If you find yourself under a financial strain, you may even be able to deduct premium payments from the cash value of the policy.

With some universal life policies, you may even be able to withdraw directly some of the cash value in your policy. Of course, you can also take a policy loan, just as you could with a whole life insurance policy. You have the flexibility to decide which course will best suit your needs.

Changing the amount of the premium or withdrawing part of the cash value of your policy will affect the rate at which the cash value accumulates. It may also reduce the size of the death benefit.

And, unlike other tax-deferred investments, any cash you withdraw from your universal life policy is considered basis-first. You won't incur a tax liability until your withdrawals exceed the total amount of the premiums you've paid into the policy. Any amount that exceeds this total will be taxed as regular income.

With many universal life policies, it is possible to structure your policy so that the invested cash value will eventually cover your premiums. You'll then have full life insurance coverage without having to pay any additional premiums as long as the cash-value account balance is sufficient to pay for the pure cost of insurance and any other expenses and charges.

There can be surrender charges if the policy is surrendered prematurely.

For investors who want the flexibility to change their premium or death benefit, a universal life insurance policy may be ideal.

The cost and availability of the type of life insurance that is appropriate for you depends on factors such as age, health, and the type and amount of insurance you need. If you are considering purchasing life insurance, consult a professional to help you explore your options.

What Are the Advantages of Variable Life Insurance?

Whole life insurance provides a solution to many of the shortcomings of term life insurance. However, after consumers demanded even more variety from the life insurance industry, insurers responded with yet another development: variable life insurance.

A Modern Alternative

Variable life insurance introduced a whole new concept to life insurance—the concept of investment control. Whereas whole life insurance provides fixed rates of return on cash value—rates that are determined by the insurance company—variable life insurance provides you with investment discretion over the cash value portion of your policy.

How Does Variable Life Insurance Work?

Variable life allows you to allocate your cash value among a variety of investment subaccounts. The premiums you pay are fixed for the life of the contract. The performance of your chosen subaccounts determines the growth of your cash value. They can also determine the value of your death benefit.

There are usually several subaccounts to choose from, including stock, bond, money market, and fixed-interest options. You can allocate your cash value as you see fit, and you can be as conservative or aggressive as you wish.

Financial Flexibility and a Guaranteed Death Benefit

Variable life offers you both the flexibility to design your own portfolio and the security of the guaranteed death benefit. As long as you pay your fixed premiums, your death benefit is guaranteed. This is not the case with universal or variable universal life insurance.

While your insurance needs will be determined by your own situation, you may want to consider variable life. The cost and availability of the type of life insurance that is appropriate for you depends on factors such as age, health, and the type and amount of insurance you need. If you are considering purchasing life insurance, consult a professional to explore your options.

Variable universal life insurance is sold only by prospectus. Please consider the investment objectives, risks, charges, expenses, and your need for death-benefit coverage carefully before investing. The prospectus, which contains this and other information about the investment company, can be obtained from your financial professional. Be sure to read the prospectus carefully before deciding whether to invest.

How Likely Am I to Need Long-Term Care?

One of the most commonly asked questions I get from clients is about long-term care. More specifically, "How likely am I to need long-term care?" If you were to suffer an illness or disability that required long-term nursing care, would you be covered? Probably not. The vast majority of Americans go through their lives reassuring themselves that it will never happen to them.

However, if past trends continue, 43 percent of those who reach the age of sixty-five may spend some time in a nursing home during the remainder of their lifetimes. Of that 43 percent, the average person stays in the nursing home for 2.5 years. And 21 percent can expect to stay for five years or more.[1]

This means that it could very well happen to you. And, while nursing-home costs vary from area to area, the average cost of a one-year stay in a nursing home is $64,200.[2] By 2015, this figure could soar to more than $98,000 per year.[3]

Who's paying for all that care? According to the Long-Term Care Financing Project at Georgetown University, nearly 40 percent of the cost is borne by the elderly and their families. Medicaid, the joint federal and state program that covers medical bills for the needy, pays a substantial portion of long-term-care costs, but usually only for those who are impoverished. Medicare does not pay much of the cost of long-term care, and so the elderly should not rely on Medicare for their long-term-care needs. Private insurance pays for only 10 percent of all nursing-care costs.[4]

Clearly, long-term-care costs pose a real problem for the elderly and their families. A long-term-care insurance policy can help preserve your accumulated wealth and provide guaranteed coverage in the event that you need long-term care. This can go far in helping to ensure a dignified, financially secure lifestyle during retirement.

Sources:

1. 2005 Field Guide, National Underwriter Company, 2005

2. The Federal Long-Term Care Insurance Program, 2005

3. Assumes 5 percent annual increases

4. Long-Term Care Financing Project, Georgetown University, 2004

6

Retirement Planning (How Early is Too Early?)

Many of my clients are concerned about retirement. Twentysomethings and sixtysomethings alike want to know if they'll have enough, how much they'll need, and, most importantly, how long it will last. In this chapter, I want to address many of these concerns with a discussion of the investment products and strategies specific to your retirement needs.

Should I Set Up a Traditional IRA?

Since they were created, traditional individual retirement accounts (IRAs) have grown in popularity with investors. IRAs offer some very attractive benefits. For many people, they offer a substantial current income-tax deduction. If you qualified in 2005, you could have made a tax-deductible contribution of $4,000 to your IRA (or, if married, you and your spouse could have made a combined contribution of $8,000). The contribution limit for 2005 through 2007 is $4,000, and it will increase to $5,000 per year ($10,000 for joint filers) in 2008.

In addition to this deduction, the assets in an IRA can grow with the taxes deferred. Over a period of years, this tax deferral can add up to quite a significant advantage. Contributions and earnings are taxed as ordinary income when they are withdrawn. In addition, withdrawals prior to age 59½ are subject to a 10 percent federal tax penalty.

Because Congress has tightened the requirements for IRAs, the number of people who qualify for a full deduction has been cut in half. Congress has also added a heavy burden of paperwork to anyone who makes nondeductible contributions to an IRA. Therefore, before you jump into an IRA, it's important for you to determine whether it will meet your retirement needs.

Will Your Contributions Be Deductible?

The first thing to determine is whether your contributions to a traditional IRA are deductible. If you are an active participant in a qualified retirement plan—such as a simplified employee pension or a 401(k) plan—your IRA deduction may have been reduced or eliminated.

For active participants in qualified plans, the IRA deduction drops by $10 for every $50 of income above the bottom figure on the phaseout ranges. Nondeductible contributions may necessitate some very complicated paperwork when you begin withdrawals. If your contributions aren't deductible, you may be better served by another kind of retirement plan.

An IRA Could Make Sense for You

If you qualify to make tax-deductible contributions and can leave your funds in place, IRAs often make sense. An IRA could be a valuable addition to your retirement and tax-planning efforts. By working with a financial advisor, you can determine whether an IRA makes sense for you.

How Does a 401(k) Plan Work?

Of all the retirement-planning options that are available, 401(k) plans are among the best for accumulating retirement funds.

Unlike a taxable savings vehicle, a 401(k) plan allows you to make annual pre-tax contributions of up to $15,000 (in 2006). And pre-tax contributions are much better for savers than after-tax contributions. For example, if you are in the 25-percent federal marginal tax bracket, it effectively costs you only $75 of spendable income to save $100 for retirement. The situation is even better for those in higher tax brackets.

Like other qualified retirement plans, a 401(k) allows your money to grow tax-deferred. This enables you to build capital significantly faster than would be the case if you were participating in similar investments outside the shelter of an employer-sponsored plan. Distributions from a 401(k) plan prior to age 59½ may be subject to a 10 percent federal tax penalty and are included in your gross income.

A 401(k) plan also offers some additional benefits that make it particularly attractive.

Portability

A 401(k) plan is portable. Unlike some other employer-sponsored retirement plans, you can take your 401(k) plan with you when you change employers.

Within certain limits, the accumulated funds in your 401(k) plan can be rolled over into your new employer's retirement plan without penalty. If your new employer's retirement plan doesn't allow such transfers, you can roll over the funds into a traditional individual retirement account.

Employer Matching

Many employers offering 401(k) plans to their employees match contributions. For example, your employer may add a certain amount for each dollar you contribute, up to a limit of a certain percentage of your salary. That's an automatic return on your investment. Over the long term, matching contributions can help you to accumulate more retirement assets than would plans based solely on employee contributions.

Investment Flexibility

A 401(k) plan can also provide a great deal of flexibility. Most 401(k) plans offer a number of investment options. This means that you're able to choose how your retirement fund will be invested. Most plans offer a stock fund, a bond fund, a money market fund, a guaranteed investment account, and company stock. You can be as aggressive or conservative as you wish.

Of course, you should remember that investments seeking higher rates of return also involve a greater degree of investment risk.

"Catch-Up" Contributions

Special "catch-up" contribution provisions enable those nearing retirement to save at an accelerated rate. Those aged fifty and older before the end of the tax year are eligible to contribute more than the regular limits. Eligible 401(k)-plan participants could contribute an additional $5,000 in 2006.

Final Analysis

If your employer offers a 401(k) plan, you should carefully weigh its benefits in light of your financial situation. A 401(k) plan can form the basis of a sound retirement-planning strategy.

What Are the Advantages of Simplified Employee Pension Plans?

Simplified employee pension (SEP) plans enable small businesses to provide retirement benefits with lower costs and less reporting requirements than other qualified retirement plans. SEPs offer some attractive benefits for employers and employees alike.

How Do SEPs Work?

A simplified employee pension plan is basically a group of individual retirement accounts maintained by employers for employees.

Under a typical SEP plan, the employer establishes IRAs for all participating employees. The employer then contributes to the IRAs, and these contributions are subject to the contribution limits for SEPs—*not* the limits of IRAs. Employer contributions are limited to 25 percent of an employee's compensation or $44,000 per year, whichever amount is lower. The company's contributions are not counted as current income for the employee.

SEP plans provide an effective retirement planning option for employees. They also provide the employer with an effective tax shelter.

The Salary-Reduction Option

Employees can also fund SEPs through pre-tax salary reduction. Under a salary-reduction SEP, or SARSEP, employees can elect to defer up to $15,000 of their annual salaries to the plan (in 2006). Employee funding further reduces costs for the employer.

This salary-reduction feature enables an SEP to work much like a 401(k) plan. Note that, as of 1996, no new SARSEP plans may be established, but contributions can continue to existing plans.

Advantages

SEPs are designed to provide a number of advantages. They feature significantly lower setup costs for employers than regular pension or profit-sharing plans. They also offer simpler reporting and record-keeping requirements.

For employees, SEPs offer substantially higher contribution limits than regular IRAs. This enables employees to accumulate more money for retirement.

The retirement benefits provided by an SEP are fully vested as soon as they are contributed. This makes them completely portable. Departing employees can roll their SEP balances into IRAs or have them transferred to retirement plans sponsored by their new employer.

Simplified employee pensions can provide significant retirement benefits to employees while minimizing setup and administrative costs for employers.

Withdrawals from SEP plans and traditional IRAs are taxed as ordinary income and, if taken out prior to age 59½, may be subject to an additional 10 percent federal tax penalty.

Should I Choose a Fixed or Variable Annuity?

Fixed and variable annuities can be important components of your long-term savings or investment portfolio. Each type of annuity has its own particular advantages and disadvantages. They also offer the potential for tax-deferred growth.

But how do you choose between them? What criteria do you use to decide whether to select a fixed annuity or a variable annuity contract?

Fixed Annuity Considerations

Fixed annuities offer tax-deferred growth. The earnings on your contract will not be taxed until they are withdrawn. This means that the capital that would ordinarily go to the tax collector can instead accumulate interest for you.

Over the life of your contract, this tax deferral can potentially make a significant difference in your earnings.

Fixed annuities offer a fixed rate of return. You know the rate of return at the beginning of each period—and that security can be very comforting.

Finally, fixed annuities offer a death benefit. If the annuitant dies before payout, his or her beneficiaries will receive all of the purchase payments plus any accumulated earnings.

Variable Annuity Considerations

Variable annuities offer many of the same benefits as fixed annuities, including tax-deferred growth and a death benefit.

Unlike with fixed annuities, however, you control where the value in your contract will be invested. Within the limits of the investment divisions, you can be as aggressive or as conservative as you like. This gives a variable annuity the potential for higher returns than a fixed annuity. But remember: this potential for higher returns requires you to assume a greater risk of loss.

Making the Choice

The type of annuity contract you choose, then, depends on what function you'd like it to perform in your savings or investment portfolio. Both fixed and variable annuities offer tax-deferred growth and a death benefit. But whereas a fixed annuity offers a fixed rate of return, a variable annuity offers some flexibility.

If you need an addition to your portfolio that offers stable, tax-deferred growth with high security, a fixed annuity could be just what you're looking for. On the other hand, if you're looking for a tax-deferred investment that will let you take a more active role, a variable annuity could be right for you. Whichever you choose, an annuity contract can be an attractive addition to your investment or savings portfolio.

Withdrawals of earnings from an annuity are taxed as ordinary income and, if taken prior to age 59½, may be subject to a 10 percent penalty. Generally, annuities contain mortality and expense charges as well as other account and administrative fees. In addition, surrender charges apply if withdrawals are made in the early years of the policy. An annuity's guarantees are contingent upon the claims-paying ability of the issuing insurance company. Variable annuity subaccounts fluctuate with changes in market conditions, and your principal, when surrendered, may be worth more or less than the original amount invested.

Variable annuities are sold only by prospectus. Please consider the investment objectives, risks, charges, and expenses carefully before investing. The prospectus, which contains this and other information about the investment company, can be obtained from your financial professional. Be sure to read the prospectus carefully before deciding whether to invest.

What About Retirement If I'm Self-Employed?

Keogh plans were created to provide a tax-sheltered retirement option for self-employed taxpayers. They can provide some very attractive tax benefits. Unlike individual retirement accounts, which limit tax-deductible contributions to $4,000 per year, Keoghs allow you to save as much as $44,000 of your net self-employment income, depending on the type of Keogh plan you adopt. Plus, you are allowed to have a Keogh plan in addition to another retirement plan such as an IRA.

The money in a Keogh plan grows tax-deferred until you withdraw it. When you make withdrawals, you can take advantage of certain tax-saving techniques—such as 10-year forward averaging—that aren't available to IRA depositors.

You can open Keogh accounts through banks, brokerage houses, insurance companies, mutual fund companies, and credit unions. Although the federal government sets no minimum opening balance, most institutions set their own—usually between $250 and $1,000. (Fees and commissions vary, so it makes sense to shop around.)

Deposit Deadline

The deposit deadline for a Keogh plan is earlier in the year than that of an IRA. You must open a Keogh by December 31 of the year for which you wish to claim a deduction. You don't have to come up with your entire contribution by then, however. As would be the case with an IRA, you don't have to deposit your contribution until the day you file your tax return. This gives most taxpayers until April 15 to deposit their annual retirement savings into a Keogh account.

Necessary Paperwork

Unfortunately, the paperwork that is required to open a Keogh account is complicated. You'll be required to fill out forms that ask very specific questions about your business, your Keogh plan's vesting schedule, and the appointment of an administrator for the plan. You may want to use the services of an accountant when filling out these forms.

Unless certain exceptions are met, Keogh owners must also file Disclosure Form 5500 or 5500-EZ annually. Some banks and brokerage houses offer their customers written advice on filling out these forms.

Whether you're self-employed either full-or part-time, a Keogh plan could be a valuable addition to your retirement strategy. And the potential payoff—a comfortable retirement—will probably be well worth the extra paperwork.

Withdrawals from Keogh plans and traditional IRAs are taxed as ordinary income and, if taken prior to age 59½, may be subject to an additional 10 percent federal tax penalty.

Back to School

Most of my clients consider providing for their children—and even their grand-children—when they plan their own retirement. Here are a few college plans I suggest that they consider:

529 Lesson Plan:

High Scores for the 529 College Savings Program

Are you looking for a tax-advantaged college savings plan that has no age restrictions, no income phaseout limits, no residency requirements—and one that you can use to pay for more than just tuition?

In that case, you should consider the 529 savings plan, which is an increasingly popular way to save for higher-education expenses. Such expenses have more than tripled over the past two decades—the average private four-year college now costs more than $29,000 per year.[1] Named after the section of the tax code that authorizes them, 529 plans (also known as qualified state tuition programs) are now offered in almost every state.

Most people have heard about the original form of 529—the state-operated prepaid tuition plan. This allows you to purchase units of future tuition at today's rates, with the plan assuming the responsibility of investing the funds to keep pace with inflation. It's practically guaranteed that the cost of an equal number of units of education in the sponsoring state will be covered, regardless of investment performance or the rate of tuition increase.

Of course, each state plan has a different set of rules and restrictions. Prepaid tuition programs typically will pay future college tuition at any of the sponsoring state's eligible colleges and universities (and some will pay an equal amount to private and out-of-state institutions).

The newer variety of 529 is the savings plan. It's similar to an investment account, but the funds accumulate tax-deferred. Withdrawals from state-sponsored 529 plans are free of federal income tax as long as they are used for qualified college expenses.[2]

Unlike the case with prepaid tuition plans, contributions can be used for all qualified higher-education expenses (tuition, fees, books, equipment, supplies, room, and board), and the funds usually can be used at all accredited post-secondary schools in the United States. The risk with these plans is that investments may lose money or may not perform well enough to cover as many college costs as had been anticipated.

In most cases, 529 savings plans place investment dollars in a mix of funds based on the age of the beneficiary, with account allocations becoming more conservative as the time for college draws closer. Recently, more states have hired professional money managers—many of them with well-known investment firms—to actively manage and market their plans. This allows a growing number of investors to customize their asset allocations.

Some states enable account owners to qualify for a deduction on their state tax returns or to receive a small matching amount on the money invested. In forty-eight states, earnings are exempt from taxes.[3] And there are even new consumer-friendly reward programs that allow people who purchase certain products and services to receive rebate dollars to be deposited into state-sponsored college savings accounts.

Funds contributed to a 529 plan are considered to be gifts to the beneficiary, so anyone—even non-relatives—can contribute up to $12,000 per year (in 2006) to a beneficiary without incurring gift-tax consequences. Contributions can be made in one lump sum or in monthly installments. Furthermore, assets contributed to a 529 plan are not considered part of the account-owner's estate, and so estate taxes are not owed on them upon the owner's death.

Major Benefits

These savings plans generally allow people of any income level to contribute, and there are no age limits for the student. The account owner can maintain control of the account until funds are withdrawn and, if desired, can even change the beneficiary as long as he or she is within the immediate family of the original beneficiary.

A 529 plan is also extremely simple to deal with when it comes to tax reporting—the sponsoring state, not you, is responsible for all income-tax recordkeeping. At the end of a year in which a withdrawal is made for college, you will receive Form 1099 from the state, and there is only one figure that you must enter on it: the amount of income reported on the student's tax return.

Benefits for Grandparents

The 529 plan is a great way for grandparents to shelter inheritance money from estate taxes and contribute substantial amounts to a student's college fund. At the same time, the grandparents also control the assets and can retain the power to control withdrawals from the account.

By accelerating use of the annual gift tax exclusion, a grandparent—or anyone, for that matter—could elect to use five years' worth of annual exclusions by making a single contribution of as much as $60,000 per beneficiary in 2006 (or a couple could contribute $120,000 in that same year) as long as no other contributions are made for that beneficiary for five years.[4] If the account's owner dies, the 529-plan balance is not considered part of his or her estate for tax purposes.

By comparing different plans, you can determine which might be best for your situation. You may find that 529 programs can make saving for college easier than you had anticipated.

Sources:

1. *The College Board*, 2005

2. As with other investments, there are generally fees and expenses associated with participation in a Section 529 savings plan. In addition, there are no guarantees regarding the performance of the underlying investments in Section 529 plans. The tax implications of a Section 529 savings plan should be discussed with your legal and/or tax advisors because they can vary significantly from state to state. Also note that most states offer their own Section 529 plans, which may provide advantages and benefits exclusively for these states' residents and taxpayers. The tax-free qualified withdrawal provision of these plans is due to expire after December 31, 2010, unless new legislation is enacted by Congress.

3. SavingForCollege.com

4. If the donor takes the five-year option and dies during the five-year calendar period, part of the contribution could revert back to the donor's estate.

Real Estate as Investment:

When Your House Is More Than a Home

Let's not forget about real estate investing. Many of my clients own property, and as they head toward retirement, they sometimes leverage that property to invest in other real estate opportunities.

To fully understand real estate, you must understand the loans needed to purchase that property. Below is a series of tables that show the advantages and disadvantages of various types of loan.

Years you plan to live in the home	Recommended program	
1-3 years	3/1 ARM, 1 year ARM or 6 month ARM	
3-5 years	5/1 ARM	
5-7 years	7/1 ARM	
7-10 years	10/1 ARM, 30 year fixed or 15 year fixed	
10+ years	30 year fixed or 15 year fixed	

Loan Program	Advantages	Disadvantages
Fixed Rate Mortgages 30 year fixed 15 year fixed	Monthly payments are fixed over the life of the loan Interest rate does not change Protected if rates go up Can refinance if rates go down	Higher interest rate Higher mortgage payments Rate does not drop if interest rates improve

Loan Program	Advantages	Disadvantages
<u>Adjustable Rate Mortgages (ARMs)</u> 10/1 ARM 7/1 ARM 5/1 ARM 3/1 ARM 1 year ARM 6 month ARM 1 month ARM	Lower initial monthly payment Rates and payments may go down if rates improve May qualify for higher loan amounts 30 year term, no balloon payment	More risk Payments may change over time Potential for higher payments if rates increase

Loan Program	Advantages	Disadvantages
Balloon Mortgages 7 year 5 year	Lower initial monthly payment Lower payment for a predetermined period of time Many balloon mortgages offer the option to convert to a new loan after the initial term	Risk of rates being higher at the end of the initial fixed period Risk of foreclosure if you cannot make a balloon payment, refinance, or exercise the conversion option Balloon payment requires you to sell or refinance after the term, as opposed to a 7/1 or 5/1 program with a 30-year term

Loan Program	Advantages	Disadvantages
First-Time Buyer Programs	Lower down payment Easier to qualify Lower rates may be available	May be subject to income and property-value limitations Some government-subsidized programs may generate a recapture tax if you sell the house too soon Education courses may be required to qualify for these loans
Loan Program	Advantages	Disadvantages
Stated Income Programs	No need to verify income Faster approval Good for borrowers who don't qualify for a full income documentation program	Higher rates Higher down payment
Loan Program	Advantages	Disadvantages
Interest-Only Programs	Several payment options Lower monthly payments Qualify for a higher loan amount Qualify at the interest only payment Option to pay the full normal payment Interest-only payments for up to ten years	Higher rates Principal loan balance will not decrease during the interest-only payment period Payment will be higher for the remaining term
Loan Program	Advantages	Disadvantages
No point, No fee Programs	No out-of-pocket loan costs at closing Closing costs are paid from the lender rebate Less money required to close Refinance without increasing your loan amount	Higher rates Higher payments Some lenders may have a short-payoff penalty which is usually charged to the loan broker, but may be passed on to you Some require a prepayment penalty for the first one to five years
Loan Program	Advantages	Disadvantages

Imperfect Credit Programs	Potential for reestablishing credit if you pay your mortgage on time When these are used for debt consolidation, you may be able to reduce your monthly debt payment	Higher rates Terms may not be as favorable Harder to get long-term fixed loans Loans may have prepayment penalties

Loan Program	Advantages	Disadvantages
Home Equity Line of Credit	You only borrow what you need Pay interest only on what you borrow Flexible access to funds Interest may be tax-deductible May be free of closing costs A good source for an emergency fund, if set up in advance Can be used for debt consolidation and lower payments Rates are usually lower than consumer-loan or credit-card rates	Rates can change. The maximum interest rate can be relatively high Payments can change Harder to refinance your first mortgage

Loan Program	Advantages	Disadvantages
Home Equity Fixed Loan	Fixed payments Interest may be tax deductible Get cash out for any purpose	Higher interest rates compared to first mortgages Harder to refinance your first mortgage Interest is paid on the entire loan amount, as opposed to an equity line of credit

What Is a Payment Option ARM Loan Program?

And Is It Right for You?

This type of loan program is an adjustable-rate mortgage with a low initial monthly payment that will increase each year for the first five years. It also offers other payment options to help you budget your monthly cash-flow

- Minimum Monthly Payment

- Interest-Only Payment

- 30-year Amortized Payment

- 40-year Amortized Payment

- 15-year Amortized Payment

Its low introductory start-rate allows you to make very low initial mortgage payments, and low qualifying rates enable you to qualify for a more expensive home.

Calculating the monthly payment

The payment schedule for the first five years starts by calculating the payment using the initial low introductory rate—usually 1 percent to 2 percent. This will be your payment rate. Each year for the first five years, the payment will increase by 7.5 percent. Here is a simple graphic to help explain:

Minimum Payment Changes		
Year 1	$1000.00	= Base of Minimum Payment
Year 2	$1075.00	= Year 1 $1000.00 + 7.50%
Year 3	$1155.63	= Year 2 $1075.00 + 7.50%
Year 4	$1242.30	= Year 3 $1155.63 + 7.50%
Year 5	$1335.47	= Year 4 $1242.30 + 7.50%

In the sixth year, the payment will be calculated using the index rate plus the margin rate, and will be amortized over the remaining term of the loan. On a thirty-year loan, the remaining term is twenty-five years. On a forty year loan, the remaining term is thirty-five years.

The "note rate" is the interest rate the bank will charge you each month. Some programs use the introductory rate as the note rate for the first three months. After that introductory period, the note rate is adjusted to the total of the index rate plus the margin rate. The following chart should help you to better understand such terms:

EXAMPLE:	COFI index	3.626
	Margin	2.250
	Index + Margin	5.876
Payment Calculation:		
Year 1	Use Introductory Rate	1.000%
	Term	30 years
	Initial Loan Amount	
Year 6	Index + Margin	5.876
	Term	25 years
	Loan Amount plus Deferred Interest	

Deferred Interest

The minimum-payment option can help keep your monthly payments affordable. If the minimum monthly payment is not sufficient to pay the monthly interest due, you will then have deferred interest. That is, the amount of interest that was not paid will be added to the principal loan balance.

Your loan balance increases each month instead of decreasing like in a normal loan. This is the source of the term "negative amortized loan." You can always avoid deferred interest by choosing the interest-only payment option.

Payment Options

With the option ARM, you generally have at least two fully amortized payment choices, which leads to a quicker loan payoff. If you prefer to pay off your loan on schedule, you can make the fully amortized payment based on a thirty-or forty-year loan, or you can choose the fifteen-year payment option for the fastest equity buildup.

Option ARM loan programs are right for you if you'd like to own your property only for a short time and would prefer your monthly payment to be affordable and flexible. However, if you select the minimum payment option in the early years, you should be prepared for possible sudden increases in your monthly payments thereafter.

Four Types of Payment Options

ARM loan programs offer a variety of payment options for your convenience, four of which I will explain for you here:

Minimum Payment

With the minimum payment option, your monthly payment is set for twelve months at your initial interest rate. After that, the payment amount changes annually.

Interest-Only Payment

With the interest-only payment option, you can avoid deferred interest when the minimum payment is not enough to pay the monthly interest due. This payment option does not result in the reduction of your principal. The interest-only payment will change every month based on changes in the ARM index used to determine your fully indexed rate.

Fully Amortized Fifteen-, Thirty-, or Forty-Year Payment

"Fully amortized" means that you have equal monthly payments for the entire term of the loan and will have a zero balance at the end. With fully amortized payments, you pay both principal and interest. Your payment is calculated each month based on the prior month's fully indexed rate, the loan balance, and the remaining loan term.

Index plus Margin

The "index" is the base rate used to determine your interest rate. Most people are familiar with the Prime rate, T-bill, or COFI. Option ARM programs are usually based on one of the following indexes:

- Monthly Treasury Average (MTA)

- London InterBank Offered Rate (LIBOR)

- 11th District Cost Of Funds Index (COFI)

- Cost of Savings Index (COSI)

The "margin" is the number of percentage points (for example, 2.75) the lender adds to the index rate to calculate the ARM interest rate, or note rate, at each adjustment. The margin is fixed at the time the loan is funded.

The interest rate you will be charged is the index rate plus the margin.

The Payment Option ARM goes by several different names: Option ARM, PayOption, Pick-a-Payment, Neg Am Variable, and Negative Amortized Loan.

Putting It All Together

I know that all this is a lot to digest. The good thing is that you have all the time in the world. Like I always say, "It's never too early to learn or too late to begin." While I hope that you begin to act sooner rather than later to secure your financial future, human nature is such that you'll only truly begin when you're *ready* to begin. If that's tomorrow, great. If that's next month, fine. If that's next year, so be it. The point is to *begin*.

You'll be happy to hear that the most difficult material is behind you. In the remaining few chapters, I'll wind down our discussion and focus less on the *how* and more on the *why*. Consider it equal parts wake-up call and call to action. I want to give you a well-rounded financial education; I want our journey to come full circle.

In the beginning stages of our journey, we got to know each other a little better, spent some time looking at the scenery and warming up the engine. By chapters 2 and 3, we were really humming along, discussing the ins and outs of investing for beginners and why it is so important. Toward the middle of our journey, we got to the nitty-gritty: investing practices, products, and procedures. Now, the end of our journey is in sight, and I'm about ready to stop the car. We'll get out and stretch our legs a bit. Then, I'll let you take the wheel.

I think you're ready, and I think I see our stop just ahead!

7

Consistency Is Key

The bottom line with investing is this: you can buy all the software, hire a crack team of financial planners, read every bestseller, and study every product currently on the market; you can do your homework, fill your journals, and cover your bulletin board with reminders to "do this" or "save that"—but if you're not ready to *commit*, you might as well have just gone to the movies.

In this book, I've tried to share with you my formula for investing wisely over time, whether you're just starting out in life or are winding down a Thirty-year career. Now, as our journey together ends and yours continues, I want to leave you with some practical advice that you can use right now—*today*. On the following pages, I'll list some very simple things you can do every day, every week, every month, and every year to better prepare yourself for the financial road that lies ahead.

My goal here is to help create habits in you, habits that can begin to stem the tide of wasteful spending, reverse the tide of never saving, or increase the tide of investing that you may have already started.

It's easy to get *temporarily* inspired to do something positive. When I was younger and the *Rocky* movies were popular, each new installment in the series would inspire me to work out, get in shape, and jog, all the while with that distinctive theme song running through my mind. The workouts, the rope-jumping, and the jogging never lasted very long. It was only later in life, when I formed good habits, that I began exercising consistently.

As I've stressed throughout this book, consistency is key. Don't let your investing be only superficially inspirational, like those *Rocky* movies. Don't get all excited just because you read this book, invest in a few products, and then let your interest in them lapse because the soundtrack faded and the theater has cleared out.

I may not be able to provide a *Rocky*-esque theme to keep you motivated as you divvy up your monthly earnings to invest, but I can point to your healthy financial future as an image that is more powerful than any special effect or movie soundtrack. When you focus on the future and realize that the decisions you make today affect every day you live past the age of sixty-two, I think you'll be sufficiently motivated to begin investing today.

How will you get there? How can you best use the days, weeks, months, and years that separate you from the future? Whatever product or combination of products you choose—be it an IRA, 401(k), mutual fund, stock, or bonds—be consistent in your strategy and your attitude. Have a plan. Don't just save when it's convenient—save *diligently*. Have a plan. Don't just talk about it, *do* it. *Have a plan.*

Only by having a clear and realistic plan and sticking to it *consistently* will you make your financial dreams come true. I've tried to show you through examples, anecdotes, products, and strategies what to do and how to do it. I'll now present you with a few final lessons that I hope you'll remember for the remainder of your financial journey.

Daily

What can you do every day to get into solid financial shape? Actually, it's easier than you think to get financially healthy. There are many tips, tricks, and tactics you can use to form good daily fiscal habits that will stand you in good stead for the rest of your life. Here are just a few:

- **Read up:** Knowledge is power. There is a lot of knowledge out there, particularly when it comes to finances. Don't try to read it all. Pick one financial journal, magazine, Web site, or newsletter that appeals to you and spend a little time each day learning from it.

- **Spend down:** Always be on the lookout for ways to decrease your spending and increase your savings. This can mean something as simple as cutting out that expensive cup of daily coffee and investing the savings from this sacrifice at the end of the month.

- **Talk it out:** Whether it's with your partner, friend, financial planner, co-worker, coach, or mentor, talk with someone every day about what you intend to do. Other people can be great resources, sounding boards, and fonts of wisdom when it comes to money. Listen to each of them with a bit of healthy skepticism, of course, but talking out loud about your plans may just be a great daily habit you can actually learn to enjoy!

- **Target one product you can do without:** A cup of coffee, a pack of cigarettes, a new CD, a book that you know will go on sale in a month—eliminate one of them from today's spending. We all spend frivolously, and we can all spend a lot less. Make it a habit to be on the lookout for items you can delete from your monthly budget.

- **Commit:** Commit to good habits. Commit to following a written plan for your future. Sign a contract with yourself and stick to it!

Weekly

The weeks of the year represent fifty-two opportunities for you to make great financial choices where your investments are concerned. My hope is that your daily habits will translate into weekly progress. Here's how you can accomplish this:

- **Be realistic:** Some habits are harder to build than others. Maybe your schedule doesn't allow you to do your financial reading every day. If a task isn't realistic, you simply won't do it. So pick one day and time each week—Wednesday night, Saturday morning, whatever—and devour an entire financial magazine instead of nibbling at it all week long.

- **Make a progress report:** Benchmarks are a great tool for checking your progress and seeking inspiration for the week ahead. Do your banking online—or use some other online product—and spend one morning, afternoon, or evening a week charting your progress. It's a great way to see where you've been, where you're going, and how you're doing right now.

- **Regroup:** From time to time during the week, you might let your good intentions slip back into bad habits. Let's say that you've decided to bring your lunch to work in order to save money. This is a great idea, but it's pretty hard to switch gears in one week. If you do "fall off the wagon" and eat out once or twice during the week, don't be too hard on yourself. Just spend a little time analyzing your temporary setback and move on to the next step.

- **Get back on track:** If your financial planning does go south during the week, don't waste time fretting about your "failure." Just get back on track for *next* week. Reschedule, recommit, and refocus. Learn from this week's setbacks what you can do better next week.

Monthly

If we plan well and remain consistent, we can do a lot in a month. On the other hand, if we give in to old habits and pay little attention to our finances, we can easily let a month slip through our fingers without doing a single positive thing for our finances. Here's how to avoid that:

- **Buy a calendar:** Calendars are one of the most inexpensive—and most effective—ways of mapping out your fiscal year. Buy one with large empty blocks for each day, so that you can write plenty in them. Sit down at the beginning of each month and think of little goals you can set for yourself throughout the month. Each time you reach a goal, circle it in red, slap a sticker onto it, or commemorate it in some other way. At the end of each month, sit down and analyze how many goals you met, then reassess your requirements before planning your goals for the following month.

- **Start thinking in dozens:** Some of us do better when we see dozens instead of hundreds. If 365 days of investing sound too daunting for, maybe twelve months of investing would sound a lot easier. Whichever works best for you, do it!

- **See the big picture:** If you find yourself stumbling over your daily or weekly goals, think bigger and give yourself monthly goals. These can be simple, like "practice with Quicken" or "open a savings account." Simple goals are still goals; small steps will still move you in the right direction.

- **Think small:** Big goals like "save more" can be meaningless if they don't have details as guidelines. I'd rather see you have a smaller, more specific goal like "save $200 this month" instead of something grand and unrealistic like "retire by the time I'm forty."

- **Give yourself the cushion of time:** Daily and weekly goals are designed to make you feel better, not worse. If they seem to be making you stumble left and right, step back and reassess—give yourself the cushion of some extra time. A month is thirty days of opportunity. When you focus on the negative instead of the positive, you can really derail an otherwise positive budget.

Yearly

Thinking in terms of years is a great way to commit to securing a brighter financial future. Unfortunately, everybody's New Year resolutions start on the same day and seem to fizzle out a week or two later. It's time to start thinking of a year as 365 consecutive days and not a timespan defined by holidays.

Your financial year starts when you make a firm commitment to improving your investments. This can be the first Tuesday of February or the last Thursday of December. If that's the day you decide to get serious about your strategies and products, then that's the day your year begins. Here is how to make the most out of your year, no matter when it starts:

- **Take the holidays off:** Every calendar should have some built-in "free time" when you can feel comfortable splurging on a luxury that you're going without on the other days of the year. A holiday—be it St. Patrick's Day or Halloween—is a good, built-in time during any year to take a break from your ledgers, go out, and have some fun!

- **Set a series of benchmarks**: I'm not suggesting that you plan out every day of your year, but that you at least give yourself some solid goals to achieve over the next twelve months. They can focus on amounts, products, strategies, or even philosophies. But if you're not actively working toward something, then all of your goals become a lot easier to forget!

- **Chart your progress:** Use one of the products we talked about (*Quicken*, *Money*, etc.) and regularly update your progress. Give yourself annual benchmarks to help you see whether all those daily, weekly, and monthly activities you're charting are actually paying off.

- **Celebrate:** Milestones are important. Giving yourself an annual goal and then actually achieving it feels good. Act accordingly!

- **Keep a financial journal:** It's important to think about investing. When we write down our thoughts about money, it can help us nurture our good habits and weed out our bad ones. I've provided your first thirty days' worth of journal space at the back of this book!

Conclusion
Kids Can Do! Or, What Can Five Empty Jars Teach Us About Our Children's Financial Future?

"Kids Can Do!" That's my motto. What, exactly, can kids do? Well, for starters, they can learn about forming good financial habits. They can also teach us a lot about what we do right—and not so right.

Now that we've come to our last chapter, I want to take some time to discuss the next generation: our children. As parents, it is incredibly important for us to make sure that our kids get a good education. And they don't just need to learn the basics of history, English, and science. They also need a solid financial education to prepare them for the modern American world of saving and spending and all that these entail.

Our education system does a great job of teaching them about the Founding Fathers and how to diagram a sentence, but it does little, if anything, to prepare them for saying no to the onslaught of media unceasingly enticing them to spend their money. It is amazing to me that, with all the subjects that are taught during our children's early years, the study of money and personal finances is not part of any curriculum I've ever heard about, let alone seen when my kids bring homework into the house.

But what is more important than understanding how to balance your checkbook, what it means to have good credit, or how to read a basic bank statement to monitor you own cash flow?

These aren't just luxuries to be taught as electives during senior skip days in high school. They are the first stepping stones toward our financial futures, and they need to be taught as early as reading, writing, and arithmetic.

If the school boards of America could see my many clients who walk into my office every day unprepared to face their financial futures, I'm sure that they would agree with me. These are doctors, lawyers, actors, politicians, parents, professionals, athletes. They are smart, intelligent, educated people whose eyes grow increasingly blank as I talk about anything having to do with debt ratios or credit allotments.

If you want something done, the old saying goes, you have to do it yourself. Never is this statement more true than when it comes to educating your children about the ins and outs of their financial futures. My wife and I teach our two boys—Chase, age eight and Chance, age five—about money, interest, real estate, savings, and many other aspects of finance. It's not always easy, and we're definitely in the minority when compared to our friends, family, co-workers, and neighbors, but it's a decision we made and a commitment we foster.

At first, I didn't think that they would understand, but kids' brains are like sponges as long as you can make a subject interesting. Therefore, I suggest that you start by playing games that reference finance and money—games like Monopoly, Cash flow for kids by Robert Kiyosaki author of rich dad, poor dad. Or even Life, which is often overlooked by modern parents (who probably played the game themselves when they were kids), but which makes references to banking, insurance policies, and even stocks and bonds.

Games can be fun and instructive, but sometimes real life is even "funner." For example, you could take the kids out on Sunday after church to open houses to help them understand about buying real estate. We've all played the "license plate game." Well, our family plays the "real estate sign game," which consists of trying to see who can find the most real estate signs on a block.

As they get comfortable with a game, and even start to look forward to it, expand on the basic rules. For example, have them guess at a price they think a house is worth. If they're anything like my five-year-old, they may at first think that it's worth a billion dollars, but once you start explaining value to them, they will scale back their estimates.

We love it when the houses in our neighborhoods have those little printouts in the plastic boxes or tubes attached to the "for sale" signs. Some of the information on these sheets is a little over their heads, but not as much as you'd think. Now they can pinpoint how many rooms a house has, how that affects price, and even how things like a garage or a pool can add tens of thousands of dollars in value to a home.

Games are great, but gains are even better. Once your children are more familiar with the various financial terms we've discussed and what they might mean, have them start creating different types of savings accounts.

Of course, going to the bank each time a child has an extra quarter can get tedious (for Mom and Dad, anyway), and piggy banks are so passé. So my wife has created little jars for the boys—five jars for each child—and, every time they receive an allowance, they divide their money into five different "accounts."

The first account is a long-term savings account, usually to save up for something that is relatively expensive. They put a portion of every allowance into this account until they reach their goal of having enough to purchase the luxury item, at which point the account is "emptied" and they start all over again.

The second jar—the next account—is a "giving account," setting aside an amount which they tithe to our church or some charity they want to give to. The third account is their "play account" (and probably their favorite). It is also their most fluid account because every week they use it to buy themselves something that they want. The fourth account is more formal—we call it their "Investing Account." They save what they can out of each allowance, and, at the end of the quarter, we take it to the bank and invest in a mutual fund in their name. Their last account is their Real Estate Long-Term Savings Account, which I hope will be able to help them with their first down payments by the time they reach the age of eighteen.

These five jars form the foundation of our children's financial education. Earlier in the book, I spoke about doing something daily, weekly, monthly, and annually to help us remain consistent and committed to our financial goals. My wife and I believe that, with these five jars, our children are already learning this consistency. Every time they get money from allowances, Christmas, birthdays, or anything else, they put it into their five jars. Of course, they are still kids, so they vary their percentage placed into each, but they always feed every jar, every week.

My hope is that these games, jars, dollars, and cents will do more than pass the time, but also help our kids form habits that will become ingrained over time. When they get older and have part-time jobs or even careers, their habits will ensure that they already have a firm grasp on the financial terms that make some of my most intelligent clients feel like they're wearing a dunce-cap.

By doing these simple things, you are teaching your children about all the things that we adults have talked about in this very book: savings, money value, goal-setting, the concept of "pay yourself first," systematic investing, real estate, and many other valuable tools that can help us all get ahead in life.

In many ways, my sons' five jars symbolize what it takes to invest successfully. We can't put all our eggs in one basket. We must diversify over time. We must remain consistent and committed to the path we've chosen if we want to reach our final destination.

We must also start *now*. We are no longer children, but we can learn like children. We, too, can treat money as a game. We may play more serious games now that we're older, but we can still set aside our own five jars to help us prioritize what we spend our money on, how much of it we need, and what to do with what's left over.

Whether you have children or not, I encourage you to use your own five jars—be they symbolic or literal—to help divvy up your investment funds. I'd rather see you concentrate on five specific areas of your finances (for now) than fifty or five hundred. When you're comfortable with your own five areas of investing, either stick to them or branch out—whatever works best for *you*.

I suppose that this is my final message. My wife and I do what works for us. My children do what works for them. All of us should do what works for ourselves to make our futures brighter, more comfortable, and less stressful.

I urge you and your family to do what works.

About the Author
Cory Chapman

Cory Chapman is currently the managing partner and CEO of Elite Financial Center, Inc. He founded this company with the expressed intent of helping people get involved with financial and insurance planning. Mr. Chapman has been named Businessman of the Year for 2004 by the NRCC business advisory council. He is also associated with Los Angeles chapter of the National Life and Underwriters Association, as well as the Certified Financial Planners Association.

He currently sits on the Mayor's Advisory Board for the City of Inglewood. He is also a board member of People Coordinated Services. He chairs the minority business development program of Los Angeles, and he founded the Elite Martial Arts Center for underprivileged children. He has been featured in many financial magazines and has been a keynote speaker at the events of many public and private organizations. He has been interviewed on both radio and television by the financial media.

Within the first two years of his financial and insurance career, he became one of the leading insurance agents in southern California. Shortly thereafter, his desires to better serve his clients led him to obtain security designations in order to enhance his clients' financial-planning goals.

Now, thirteen years later, Mr. Chapman has managed over $75-million in assets and is currently building a financial center that will be able to handle every financial situation that a client may have—a financial "one-stop shop." He has hired some of the best and brightest in the industry, and his company now specializes in many areas.

Contact information:
300 Corporate Point, Suite 400
Culver City, CA 90230
Office: 310-645-2345
Fax: 310-645-2525
Email: cory@financialcenter.com
URL: www.efcfinancialcenter.com

Resources

Your 30-Day Personal Finance Journal

Thoughts for Making Every Penny Count!

In school, I was told the same thing year after year: "Don't write in your book!" The teacher looked at our textbooks at the beginning of the year and again at the end, carefully scrutinizing each page from the Table of Contents to the Index, all to see if we'd doodled our names or drawn moustaches on George Washington's face.

I certainly hope you've learned something in these pages, but this is not a schoolbook. I want you to write in this book as much as my former teachers wanted me *not* to write in theirs. For that reason, I've included a complimentary 30-Day Personal Finance Journal just for you.

It's not like some other journals, which don't have much room for you to write down your innermost thoughts. I've made sure that there are plenty of lines and more than enough room for you to doodle all day long, if that's what helps you toward your goals, dreams, and financial desires.

And don't worry: nobody else will ever read it, grade it, or judge it. Indulging your freedom of expression is the only real way for you to answer life's toughest questions or celebrate your strongest, deepest desires. Therefore, I want you to feel free to write exactly what you feel and remain safe in the knowledge that your thoughts, feelings, and emotions are for your eyes only and not for public scrutiny.

I realize this can be a difficult, disconcerting, and even threatening time. Money changes people—both the lack of it and the amassing of it. Perhaps you've already started saving money, or maybe you've dabbled with investing in a stock or two. Perhaps you've even gone on a two-week spending binge knowing that this moment—the end of this book—means the end of all that.

Whatever your situation, we've talked about a lot here but mostly it's been you listening to me. Now I want it to be your turn—your turn to talk, rant, rave, question, calculate, plan, solve, achieve, budget, spend, eliminate, and add.

It's not difficult, but it's quite constructive. I have stacks of these blank journals lying around my office and pass them out to clients on our first consultation. Believe it or not, I even keep a journal like this for myself and have found it quite useful over the years. It's quite simple: each day begins with a problem and ends with a solution. You choose a problem, think about them a little—out loud or on paper—and eventually arrive at its solution.

For example, your problem of the day might be, "I feel like I'm leaking money, and I don't know where to plug the leak!" That's a common problem but one with a myriad of solutions. In fact, your solution might be something as simple as, "I started paying all my bills online today and calculated that this will save me at least $200 a year in postage!"

After each solution, I've provided space for you to write down any general feelings, tactics, emotions, or concerns you might have in the solution's wake. Personally, I use this space to set myself up for the next day's problem. But it's a "free space," and you should feel comfortable using it in any way you see fit.

This goes for the journal as a whole. It lasts a full month because I find that it usually takes my clients at least thirty days to experience any real, lasting change in their habits. A whole month gives you the time to truly absorb what you've read here and apply it to your own life.

So, what are you waiting for?

It's time for you to start listening to your teacher and writing in your book!

Name: _____

DAY 1

Date: __/__/__ __

Problem of the Day: _____
_____
_____
_____

Solution of the Day: _____
_____
_____
_____

General Thoughts: _____
_____
_____
_____
_____
_____
_____
_____
_____

DAY 2

Date: __/__/_ _

Problem of the Day: _____
_____
_____
_____

Solution of the Day: _____
_____
_____
_____

General Thoughts: _____
_____
_____
_____
_____
_____
_____
_____
_____

DAY 3

Date: __/_/_ _

Problem of the Day: _____
_____
_____
_____

Solution of the Day: _____
_____
_____
_____

General Thoughts: _____
_____
_____
_____
_____
_____
_____
_____

DAY 4

Date: __/__/__ __

Problem of the Day: _____
_____
_____
_____

Solution of the Day: _____
_____
_____
_____

General Thoughts: _____
_____
_____
_____
_____
_____
_____
_____
_____

DAY 5

Date: __/_/_ _

Problem of the Day: _____
_____
_____
_____

Solution of the Day: _____
_____
_____
_____

General Thoughts: _____
_____
_____
_____
_____
_____
_____
_____
_____

DAY 6

Date: __/__/__ __

Problem of the Day: _____
_____
_____
_____

Solution of the Day: _____
_____
_____
_____

General Thoughts: _____
_____
_____
_____
_____
_____
_____
_____
_____

DAY 7

Date: __/__/_ _

Problem of the Day: _____
_____
_____
_____

Solution of the Day: _____
_____
_____
_____

General Thoughts: _____
_____
_____
_____
_____
_____
_____
_____
_____

DAY 8

Date: __/__/__ __

Problem of the Day: _____
_____
_____
_____

Solution of the Day: _____
_____
_____
_____

General Thoughts: _____
_____
_____
_____
_____
_____
_____
_____
_____

DAY 9

Date: __/__/_ _

Problem of the Day: _____

_____

_____

_____

Solution of the Day: _____

_____

_____

_____

General Thoughts: _____

_____

_____

_____

_____

_____

_____

_____

DAY 10

Date: __/__/_ _

Problem of the Day: _____
_____
_____
_____

Solution of the Day: _____
_____
_____
_____

General Thoughts: _____
_____
_____
_____
_____
_____
_____
_____
_____

DAY 11

Date: __/_/_ _

Problem of the Day: _____
_____
_____
_____

Solution of the Day: _____
_____
_____
_____

General Thoughts: _____
_____
_____
_____
_____
_____
_____
_____
_____

DAY 12

Date: __/__/__ __

Problem of the Day: _____
_____
_____
_____

Solution of the Day: _____
_____
_____
_____

General Thoughts: _____
_____
_____
_____
_____
_____
_____
_____
_____

DAY 13

Date: __/__/__ _

Problem of the Day: _____
_____
_____
_____

Solution of the Day: _____
_____
_____
_____

General Thoughts: _____
_____
_____
_____
_____
_____
_____
_____

DAY 14

Date: __/_/_ _

Problem of the Day: _____

_____

_____

_____

Solution of the Day: _____

_____

_____

_____

General Thoughts: _____

_____

_____

_____

_____

_____

_____

_____

_____

DAY 15

Date: __/__/___

Problem of the Day: _____
_____
_____
_____

Solution of the Day: _____
_____
_____
_____

General Thoughts: _____
_____
_____
_____
_____
_____
_____
_____

DAY 16

Date: __/_/_ _

Problem of the Day: _____

_____

_____

_____

Solution of the Day: _____

_____

_____

_____

General Thoughts: _____

_____

_____

_____

_____

_____

_____

_____

_____

DAY 17

Date: __/__/____

Problem of the Day: _____
_____
_____
_____

Solution of the Day: _____
_____
_____
_____

General Thoughts: _____
_____
_____
_____
_____
_____
_____
_____
_____
_____

DAY 18

Date: __/_/_ _

Problem of the Day: _____
_____
_____
_____

Solution of the Day: _____
_____
_____
_____

General Thoughts: _____
_____
_____
_____
_____
_____
_____
_____
_____

DAY 19

Date: __/_/_ _

Problem of the Day: _____

_____

_____

_____

Solution of the Day: _____

_____

_____

_____

General Thoughts: _____

_____

_____

_____

_____

_____

_____

_____

DAY 20

Date: __/__/____

Problem of the Day: _____
_____
_____
_____

Solution of the Day: _____
_____
_____
_____

General Thoughts: _____
_____
_____
_____
_____
_____
_____
_____
_____

DAY 21

Date: __/__/__ __

Problem of the Day: _____

_____

_____

_____

Solution of the Day: _____

_____

_____

_____

General Thoughts: _____

_____

_____

_____

_____

_____

_____

_____

_____

DAY 22

Date: __/_/_ _

Problem of the Day: _____
_____
_____
_____

Solution of the Day: _____
_____
_____
_____

General Thoughts: _____
_____
_____
_____
_____
_____
_____
_____
_____
_____

DAY 23

Date: __/_/_ _

Problem of the Day: _____
_____
_____
_____

Solution of the Day: _____
_____
_____
_____

General Thoughts: _____
_____
_____
_____
_____
_____
_____
_____

DAY 24

Date: __/__/__ __

Problem of the Day: _____
_____
_____
_____

Solution of the Day: _____
_____
_____
_____

General Thoughts: _____
_____
_____
_____
_____
_____
_____
_____
_____

DAY 25

Date: __/_/_ _

Problem of the Day: _____
_____
_____
_____

Solution of the Day: _____
_____
_____
_____

General Thoughts: _____
_____
_____
_____
_____
_____
_____
_____
_____

DAY 26

Date: __/_/_ _

Problem of the Day: _____
_____
_____
_____

Solution of the Day: _____
_____
_____
_____

General Thoughts: _____
_____
_____
_____
_____
_____
_____
_____
_____

DAY 27

Date: __/__/__ __

Problem of the Day: _____
_____
_____
_____

Solution of the Day: _____
_____
_____
_____

General Thoughts: _____
_____
_____
_____
_____
_____
_____
_____

DAY 28

Date: __/__/__ __

Problem of the Day: _____
_____
_____
_____

Solution of the Day: _____
_____
_____
_____

General Thoughts: _____
_____
_____
_____
_____
_____
_____
_____
_____

DAY 29

Date: __/_/_ _

Problem of the Day: _____
_____
_____
_____

Solution of the Day: _____
_____
_____
_____

General Thoughts: _____
_____
_____
_____
_____
_____
_____
_____
_____
_____

DAY 30

Date: __/__/__ __

Problem of the Day: _____
_____
_____
_____

Solution of the Day: _____
_____
_____
_____

General Thoughts: _____
_____
_____
_____
_____
_____
_____
_____
_____

Appendix
Resources for Your
Financial Future

For Your Financial Bookshelf:

Recommended Reading

I've heard it said that "education is the foundation for future prosperity." Don't let your education end with the last few pages of this book. Below is a selection of my favorite finance books. Don't forget to add your own as you continue your personal finance education.

- *The Number: A Completely Different Way to Think About the Rest of Your Life* by Lee Eisenberg

- *Why We Want You to Be Rich:* **Two Men—One Message** *by Donald Trump, Robert T. Kiyosaki, Sharon Lechter, Meredith McIver*

- Rich Dad, Poor Dad: *What the Rich Teach Their Kids about Money—That the Poor and Middle Class Do Not!* by Robert T. Kiyosaki, Sharon L. Lechter, Sharon L. Lechter, Sharon L. Lechter

- *Missed Fortune: Dispel the Money Myth-Conceptions—Isn't It Time You Became Wealthy? by Douglas R. Andrew*

- *Jim Cramer's Mad Money: Watch TV, Get Rich by James J. Cramer, Cliff Mason, Cliff Mason*

- *The Total Money Makeover: A Proven Plan for Financial Fitness* by Dave Ramsey

- *The Budget Kit: The Common Cents Money Management Workbook* by Judy Lawrence

- *The Gospel Truth About Money Management: Making Every Dollar Count* by Judy Woodward Bates

- *The Motley Fool—You Have More Than You Think: The Foolish Guide To Personal Finance* by David Gardner

- *Unconventional Success: A Fundamental Approach to Personal Investment* by David F. Swenson

Glossary

Below is a list of terms you might like to familiarize yourself with as you continue to educating yourself about today's various investment opportunities. By no means is this a complete list, but it is the one I offer clients during our early meetings, and it is usually very helpful! As you grow and learn along your investment journey, please feel free to add to it.

A

- **Adjusted Gross Income (AGI):** An interim calculation in the computation of income tax liability. It is computed by subtracting certain allowable adjustments from gross income.

- **Administrator:** A person appointed by the court to settle an estate when there is no will.

- **After-Tax Return:** The return from an investment after the effects of taxes have been taken into account.

- **Aggressive Growth Fund:** A mutual fund whose primary investment objective is substantial capital gains.

- **Alternative Minimum Tax:** A method of calculating income tax that disallows certain deductions, credits, and exclusions. This was intended to ensure that individuals, trusts, and estates that benefit from tax preferences do not escape all federal income tax liability. People must calculate their taxes both ways and pay the greater of the two.

- **Annuity:** An insurance-based contract that provides future payments at regular intervals in exchange for current premiums. Annuity contracts are usually purchased from banks, credit unions, brokerage firms, or insurance companies.

- **Asset:** Anything owned that has monetary value.

- **Asset Allocation:** The process of repositioning assets within a portfolio to maximize return for a given level of risk. This process is usually done using the historical performance of the asset classes within sophisticated mathematical models.

- **Asset Class:** A category of investments with similar characteristics.

- **Audit:** The examination of the accounting and financial documents of a firm by an objective professional. The audit is done to determine the records' accuracy, consistency, and conformity to legal and accounting principles.

B

- **Balanced Mutual Fund:** A mutual fund whose objective is a balance of stocks and bonds. Such funds tend to be less volatile than stock-only funds.

- **Bear Market:** When the stock market appears to be declining overall, it is said to be a bear market.

- **Beneficiary:** A person named in a life insurance policy, annuity, will, trust, or other agreement to receive a financial benefit upon the death of the owner. A beneficiary can be an individual, company, organization, or other entity.

- **Blue Chip Stock:** The common stock of a company with a long history of profitability and consistent dividend payments.

- **Bond:** A bond is evidence of a debt in which the issuer promises to pay the bondholders a specified amount of interest and to repay the principal at maturity. Bonds are usually issued in multiples of $1,000.

- **Book Value:** The net value of a company's assets, less its liabilities and the liquidation price of its preferred issues. The net asset value divided by the number of shares of common stock outstanding equals the book value per share, which may be higher or lower than the stock's market value.

- **Bull Market:** When the stock market appears to be advancing overall, it is said to be a bull market.

- **Buy-Sell Agreement:** A buy-sell agreement is an arrangement between two or more parties that obligates one party to buy a business and another party to sell it upon the death, disability, or retirement of one of the other owners.

C

- **Capital Gain or Loss:** The difference between the sale price and the purchase price of a capital asset. When that difference is positive, the difference is referred to as a capital gain. When the difference is negative, it is a capital loss.

- **Cash Equivalents:** Short-term investments, such as U.S. Treasury securities, certificates of deposit, and money market fund shares, that can be readily converted into cash.

- **Cash Surrender Value:** The amount that an insurance policyholder is entitled to receive when he or she discontinues coverage. Policyholders are usually able to borrow against the surrender value of a policy from the insurance company. Loans that are not repaid will reduce the policy's death benefit.

- **CERTIFIED FINANCIAL PLANNER® Practitioner:** A credential granted by the Certified Financial Planner Board of Standards, Inc., (Denver, CO) to individuals who complete a comprehensive curriculum in financial planning and ethics. CFP®, CERTIFIED FINANCIAL PLANNER®, and the federally registered CFP (with flame logo)® are certification marks owned by the Certified Financial Planner Board of Standards. These marks are awarded to individuals who successfully complete the CFP Board's initial and ongoing certification.

- **Certified Public Accountant (CPA):** A professional license granted by a state board of accountancy to an individual who has passed the Uniform CPA Examination (administered by the American Institute of Certified Public Accountants) and has fulfilled that state's educational and professional experience requirements for certification.

- **Charitable Lead Trust:** A trust established for the benefit of a charitable organization under which the charitable organization receives income from an asset for a set number of years or for the truster's lifetime. Upon the termination of the trust, the asset reverts to the truster or to his or her designated heirs. This type of trust can reduce estate taxes and allows the truster's heirs to retain control of the assets.

- **Charitable Remainder Trust:** A trust established for the benefit of a charitable organization under which the truster receives income from an asset for a set number of years or for the truster's lifetime. Upon the termination of the trust, the asset reverts to the charitable organization. The truster receives a charitable contribution deduction in the year in which the trust is established, and the assets placed in the trust are exempt from capital gains tax.

- **Chartered Financial Consultant (ChFC):** A professional financial planning designation granted by The American College (Bryn Mawr, PA) to individuals who complete a comprehensive curriculum in financial planning. Prerequisites include passing a series of written examinations, meeting specified experience requirements, and maintaining ethical standards. The curriculum encompasses wealth accumulation, risk management, income taxation, planning for retirement needs, investments, and estate and succession planning.

- **Chartered Life Underwriter (CLU):** A professional designation granted by The American College to individuals who complete a comprehensive curriculum focused primarily on risk management. Prerequisites include passing a series of written examinations, meeting specified experience requirements, and maintaining ethical standards. The curriculum encompasses insurance and financial planning, income taxation, individual life insurance, life insurance law, estate and succession planning, and planning for business owners and professionals.

- **COBRA:** The Consolidated Omnibus Budget Reconciliation Act is a federal law requiring employers with more than twenty employees to offer terminated or retired employees the opportunity to continue their health insurance coverage for eighteen additional months at the employee's expense. Coverage may be extended to the employee's dependents for thirty-six months in the case of divorce or death of the employee.

- **Coinsurance or Co-Payment:** The amount an insured person must pay for a covered medical and/or dental expense if his or her insurance doesn't provide 100 percent coverage.

- **Commodities:** The generic term for goods such as grains, foodstuffs, livestock, oils, and metals which are traded on national exchanges. These exchanges deal in both "spot" trading (for current delivery) and "futures" trading (for delivery in future months).

- **Common Stock:** A unit of ownership in a corporation. Common stockholders participate in the corporation's profits or losses by receiving dividends and by capital gains or losses in the stock's share price.

- **Community Property:** State laws vary, but generally all property acquired during a marriage—excluding property one spouse receives from a will, inheritance, or gift—is considered community property, and each partner is entitled to one-half of it. This includes debt accumulated. There are currently nine community-property states: Arizona, California, Idaho, Louisiana, Nevada, New Mexico, Texas, Washington, and Wisconsin.

- **Compound Interest:** Interest that is computed on the total amount of the principal and the accrued interest. Compound interest may be computed continuously, daily, monthly, quarterly, semiannually, or annually.

- **Consumer Price Index:** The U.S. Department of Labor's main indicator of inflation. The Consumer Price Index is calculated each month using the costs of some 400 retail items in urban areas throughout the United States.

D

- **Deduction:** An amount that can be subtracted from gross income, from a gross estate, or from a gift, thereby lowering the amount on which tax is assessed.

- **Defined Benefit Plan:** A qualified retirement plan under which a retiring employee receives a guaranteed retirement fund, usually payable in installments. Annual contributions may be made to the plan by the employer at the level needed to fund the benefit. The annual contributions are limited to a specified amount, indexed for inflation.

- **Defined Contribution Plan:** A retirement plan under which the annual contributions made by the employer or employee are generally stated as a fixed percentage of the employee's compensation or company profits. The amount of retirement benefits is not guaranteed; rather, it depends upon the investment performance of the employee's account.

- **Diversification:** Investing in different companies, industries, or asset classes. Diversification may also refer to the participation of a large corporation in a wide range of business activities.

- **Dividend:** A pro rata portion of earnings distributed in cash by a corporation to its stockholders. In preferred stock, dividends are usually fixed; with common shares, dividends may vary with the fortunes of the company.

- **Dollar Cost Averaging:** A system of investing in which the investor buys a fixed dollar amount of securities at regular intervals. The investor thus buys more shares when the price is low and fewer shares when it rises, and the average cost per share is lower than the average price per share. This strategy does not protect against loss in declining markets and involves continuous invest-ments, regardless of fluctuating price levels.

E

- **Efficient Frontier:** A statistical result from the analysis of the risk and return for a given set of assets that indicates the balance of assets that may, under cer-tain assumptions, achieve the best return for a given level of risk.

- **Employer-Sponsored Retirement Plan:** A tax-favored retirement plan that is sponsored by an employer. Among the more common employer-sponsored retirement plans are 401(k) plans, 403(b) plans, simplified employee pension plans, and profit-sharing plans.

- **Equity:** The value of a person's ownership in real property or securities; the market value of a property or business, less all claims and liens upon it.

- **ERISA:** The Employee Retirement Income Security Act is a federal law cover-ing all aspects of employee retirement plans. If employers provide plans, they must be adequately funded and provide for vesting, survivor's rights, and dis-closures.

- **ESOP (employee stock ownership plan):** A defined contribution retirement plan in which company contributions must be invested primarily in qualifying employer securities.

- **Estate Conservation:** Activities coordinated to provide for the orderly and cost-effective distribution of an individual's assets at the time of his or her death. Estate conservation often includes wills and trusts.

- **Estate Tax:** Upon the death of a decedent, federal and state governments impose taxes on the value of the estate left to others (with limitations).

- **Executive Bonus Plan:** The employer pays for a benefit that is owned by the executive. The bonus could take the form of cash, automobiles, life insurance, or other items of value to the executive.

- **Executor:** A person named by a probate court or will to carry out the direc-tions and requests of a decedent.

F

- **Fixed Income:** Income from investments such as CDs, Social Security benefits, pension benefits, some annuities, or most bonds, that is the same every month.

- **401(k) Plan:** A defined contribution plan that may be established by a company for retirement. Employees may allocate a portion of their salaries into this plan, and contributions are excluded from their income for tax purposes (with limitations). Contributions and earnings will compound tax-deferred. Withdrawals from a 401(k) plan are taxed as ordinary income and may be subject to an additional 10 percent federal tax penalty if withdrawn prior to age 59 and a half.

- **403(b) Plan:** A defined contribution plan that may be established by a non-profit organization or school for retirement. Employees may allocate a portion of their salaries to this plan, and contributions are excluded from their income for tax purposes (with limitations). Contributions and earnings will compound tax deferred. Withdrawals from a 403(b) plan are taxed as ordinary income and may be subject to an additional 10 percent federal tax penalty if withdrawn prior to age 59 and a half.

- **Fundamental Analysis:** An approach to the stock market in which specific factors—such as the price-to-earnings ratio, yield, or return on equity—are used to determine which stocks may be favorable for investment.

G

- **Gift Tax:** A federal tax levied on the transfer of property as a gift. This tax is paid by the donor. The first $12,000 a year from a donor to each recipient is exempt from tax. Most states also impose a gift tax. The gift tax exemption is indexed annually for inflation.

H

- **Holographic Will:** A will entirely in the handwriting of the testator. Without witnesses, holographic wills are valid and enforceable only in some states.

I

- **Index:** A calculation that uses a selection of stocks or bonds to gauge a certain market. The Dow Jones Industrial Average, for example, is an index of thirty large industrial companies on the New York Stock Exchange.

- **Individual Retirement Account (IRA):** Contributions to a traditional IRA are deductible from earned income in the calculation of federal and state income taxes if the taxpayer meets certain requirements. The earnings accumulate tax-deferred until withdrawn, and then they are taxed as ordinary income. Individuals not eligible to make deductible contributions may make nondeductible contributions, the earnings on which would be tax-deferred.

- **Inflation:** An increase in the price of products and services over time. The government's main measure of inflation is the Consumer Price Index.

- **Intestate:** The condition of an estate left by a decedent without a valid will. In such a situation, state laws determine who inherits the property or serves as guardian for any minor children.

- **Investment Category:** A broad class of assets with similar characteristics. The five investment categories include cash equivalents, fixed principal, equity, debt, and tangibles.

- **Irrevocable Trust:** A trust that may not be modified or terminated by the truster after its creation.

J

- **Joint and Survivor Annuity:** Most pension plans must offer this form of pension plan payout that pays over the life of the retiree and his or her spouse after the retiree dies. The retiree and his or her spouse must specifically choose not to accept this payment form if it is not desired.

- **Joint Tenancy:** Co-ownership of property by two or more people in which the survivor(s) automatically assumes ownership of a decedent's interest.

- **Jointly Held Property:** Property owned by two or more persons under joint tenancy, tenancy in common, or, in some states, community property.

K

- **Keogh Plan:** This retirement plan, named for Eugene Keogh, is designed for self-employed individuals. Up to $44,000 of self-employed income may be deducted from compensation and set aside into the plan.

L

- **Liability:** Any claim against the assets of a person or corporation. For example: accounts payable, wages and salaries payable, dividends declared payable, accrued taxes payable, and fixed or long-term obligations such as mortgages, debentures, and bank loans.

- **Limited Partnership:** Limited partnerships pool the money of investors to develop or purchase income-producing properties. When the partnership subsequently receives income from these properties, it distributes the income to its investors as dividend payments.

- **Liquidity:** The ease with which an asset or security can be converted into cash without loss of principal.

- **Living Trust:** A trust created by a person during his or her lifetime.

- **Lump-Sum Distribution:** The disbursement of the entire value of a profit-sharing plan, pension plan, annuity, or similar account to the account owner or beneficiary. Lump-sum distributions may be rolled over into another tax-deferred account.

M

- **Marginal Tax Bracket:** The range of taxable income that is taxable at a certain rate. Currently, there are six marginal tax brackets: 10 percent, 15 percent, 25 percent, 28 percent, 33 percent, and 35 percent.

- **Marital Deduction:** A provision of tax codes that allows all assets of a deceased spouse to pass to the surviving spouse free of estate taxes. This provision is also referred to as the unlimited marital deduction.

- **Money Market Fund:** A mutual fund that specializes in investing in short-term securities and that tries to maintain a constant net asset value of $1.00.

- **Municipal Bond:** A kind of debt security issued by municipalities. The income from municipal bonds is usually exempt from federal income taxes. In many states, it is also exempt from state income taxes in the state in which the municipal bond is issued.

- **Municipal Bond Fund:** A mutual fund that specializes in investing in municipal bonds.

- **Mutual Fund:** A collection of stocks, bonds, or other securities purchased and managed by an investment company with funds from a group of investors.

N

- **Net Asset Value:** The price at which a mutual fund sells or redeems its shares. The net asset value is calculated by dividing the net market value of the fund's assets by the number of outstanding shares.

P

- **Pooled Income Fund:** A trust created by a charitable organization that combines the contributions of several donors and distributes income to those donors based on the earnings of the trust. The trust is managed by the charitable organization, and contributions are partially deductible for income-tax purposes.

- **Portfolio:** All the investments held by an individual or a mutual fund.

- **Preferred Stock:** A class of stock with claim to a company's earnings before payment can be made on the common stock, and that is usually entitled to priority over common stock if the company liquidates. Generally, preferred stocks pay dividends at a fixed rate.

- **Prenuptial Agreement:** A legal agreement arranged before marriage stating who owns property acquired before marriage and during marriage and how property will be divided in the event of divorce. ERISA benefits are not affected by prenuptial agreements.

- **Price/Earnings Ratio (P/E Ratio):** The market price of a stock divided by the company's annual earnings per share. Because the P/E ratio is a widely regarded yardstick for investors, it often appears alongside stock price quotations.

- **Principal:** In a security, the principal is the original amount of money that is invested, excluding earnings. In a debt instrument such as a bond, it is the face amount.

- **Probate:** The court-supervised process in which a decedent's estate is settled and distributed.

- **Profit-Sharing Plan:** An agreement under which employees share in the profits of their employer. The company makes annual contributions to the employees' accounts. These funds usually accumulate tax-deferred until the employee retires or leaves the company.

- **Prospectus:** A document provided by mutual fund companies to prospective investors. The prospectus gives information needed by investors to make informed decisions prior to investing in a specific mutual fund. The prospectus includes information on the minimum investment amount, the fund's objectives, past performance, risk level, sales charges, management fees, and any other expense information about the fund, as well as a description of the services provided to investors in the fund.

Q

- **Qualified Domestic Relations Order (QDRO):** At the time of divorce, this order would be issued by a state domestic relations court and would require that an employee's ERISA retirement plan accrued benefits be divided between the employee and the spouse.

- **Qualified Retirement Plan:** A pension, profit-sharing, or qualified savings plan that is established by an employer for the benefit of employees. These plans must be established in conformity with IRS rules. Contributions accumulate tax-deferred until withdrawn and are deductible to the employer as a current business expense.

R

- **Revocable Trust:** A trust in which the creator reserves the right to modify or terminate the trust.

- **Risk:** The chance that an investor will lose all or part of an investment.

- **Risk Aversion:** Refers to the assumption that rational investors will choose the security with the least risk if they can maintain the same return. As the level of risk goes up, so must the expected return on the investment.

- **Rollover:** A method by which an individual can transfer assets from one retirement program to another without the recognition of income for tax purposes. The requirements for a rollover depend on the type of program from which the distribution is made and the type of program receiving the distribution.

- **Roth IRA:** A nondeductible IRA that allows tax-free withdrawals when certain conditions are met. Income and contribution limits apply.

S

- **Security:** Evidence of an investment, either in direct ownership (as with stocks), creditorship (as with bonds), or indirect ownership (as with options).

- **Simplified Employee Pension Plan (SEP):** A type of plan under which an employer contributes to an employee's IRA. Contributions may be made up to a certain limit and are immediately vested.

- **Single-Life Annuity:** An insurance-based contract that provides future payments at regular intervals in exchange for current premiums. It is generally used as a supplement to retirement income and pays over the life of one individual, usually the retiree, with no rights of payment to any survivor.

- **Split-Dollar Plan:** An arrangement under which two parties (usually a corporation and employee) share the cost of a life insurance policy and split the proceeds.

- **Spousal IRA:** An IRA designed for a couple when one spouse has no earned income. The maximum combined contribution that can be made each year to an IRA and a spousal IRA is $8,000 (in 2005 through 2007) or 100 percent of earned income, whichever is less. This total may be split between the two IRAs as the couple wishes, provided the contribution to either IRA does not exceed $4,000.

T

- **Tax Bracket:** The range of taxable income that is taxed at a certain rate. Brackets are expressed by their marginal rate.

- **Tax Credit:** Tax credits, the most appealing type of tax deductions, are subtracted directly, dollar for dollar, from your income tax bill.

- **Tax Deferral:** Allowing interest, dividends, or capital gains to grow untaxed in certain accounts or plans until the funds are withdrawn.

- **Tax-Exempt Bonds:** Under certain conditions, the interest from bonds issued by states, cities, and certain other government agencies is exempt from federal income taxes. In many states, the interest from tax-exempt bonds will also be exempt from state and local income taxes.

- **Taxable Income:** The amount of income used to compute tax liability. It is determined by subtracting adjustments, itemized deductions or the standard deduction, and personal exemptions from gross income.

- **Technical Analysis:** An approach to investing in stocks in which a stock's past performance is mapped onto charts. These charts are examined to find familiar patterns to use as an indicator of the stock's future performance.

- **Tenancy in Common:** A form of co-ownership. Upon the death of a co-owner, his or her interest passes to his or her chosen beneficiaries and not to the surviving owner or owners.

- **Term Insurance:** Term life insurance provides a death benefit if the insured party dies. Term insurance does not accumulate cash value and ends after a certain number of years or at a certain age.

- **Testamentary Trust:** A trust established by a will that takes effect upon the testator's death.

- **Testator:** One who has made a will or who dies having left a will.

- **Total Return:** The total of all earnings from a given investment, including dividends, interest, and any capital gain.

- **Trust:** A legal entity created by an individual in which one person or institution holds the right to manage property or assets for the benefit of someone else. Types of trusts include: testamentary trust—a trust established by a will that takes effect upon death; living trust—a trust created by a person during his or her lifetime; revocable trust—a trust in which the creator reserves the right to modify or terminate the trust; and irrevocable trust—a trust that may not be modified or terminated by the truster after its creation

- **Trustee:** An individual or institution appointed to administer a trust for its beneficiaries.

- **Trustee-to-Trustee Transfer:** A method of transferring retirement plan assets from one employer's plan to another employer plan or to an IRA. One benefit of this method is that no federal income tax will be withheld by the trustee of the first plan.

U

- **Universal Life Insurance:** A type of life insurance that combines a death benefit with a savings element which accumulates tax-deferred at current interest rates. Under a universal life insurance policy, a policyholder can increase or decrease his or her coverage, with limitations, without purchasing a new policy.

V

- **Variable Universal Life Insurance:** A type of life insurance that combines a death benefit with a savings element that accumulates tax-deferred at current interest rates. Under a variable universal life insurance policy, the cash value in the policy can be placed in a variety of subaccounts with different investment objectives. The policyholder can transfer funds among the subaccounts as he or she wishes. Fees are charged after a certain number of transfers.

- **Volatility:** The range of price swings of a security or market over time.

W

- **Welfare Benefit Plan:** An employee benefit plan that provides such benefits as medical, sickness, accident, disability, death, or unemployment benefits.

- **Whole Life Insurance:** A type of life insurance that offers a death benefit and also accumulates cash value, tax-deferred, at fixed interest rates. Whole life insurance policies generally have a fixed annual premium that does not rise over the duration of the policy. Whole life insurance is also referred to as "ordinary" or "straight" life insurance.

- **Will:** A legal document that declares a person's wishes concerning the disposition of property, the guardianship of his or her children, and the administration of the estate after his or her death.

Y

- **Yield:** In general, the yield is the amount of current income provided by an investment. For stocks, the yield is calculated by dividing the total of the annual dividends by the current price. For bonds, the yield is calculated by dividing the annual interest by the current price. The yield is distinguished from the return, which includes price appreciation or depreciation.

Z

- **Zero-Coupon Bond:** This type of bond makes no periodic interest payments but instead is sold at a steep discount from its face value. Bondholders receive the face value of their bonds when the bonds mature.

978-0-595-42454-2
0-595-42454-6